AFTER SOME YEARS

GW00715921

Carlo Cardinal Martini

AFTER SOME YEARS
Reflections on the ministry of the priest

VERITAS

Published 1991 by
Veritas Publications
7-8 Lower Abbey Street
Dublin 1

Italian edition first published 1987 by
Editions Piemme
15033 Casale Monferrato
Italy

ISBN 1 85390 038 9

Translation: Teresa Cadamartori
Cover design: Banahan McManus
Typesetting: Printset & Design Ltd, Dublin
Printed in the Republic of Ireland by
the Leinster Leader Ltd

Contents

Introduction

We praise you, we bless you and we thank you, Lord, because you have gathered us here from various parts of the world and, above all, from our parishes and oratories. You know that it is always difficult to separate ourselves from the habitual commitments of ministry, to liberate ourselves from the worries and problems which assail us. We want to confide everything to you, Lord, asking you for the gift of living these days of retreat with courage, overcoming every repugnance, every mistrust, every reluctance to respond to your call. From your hands we await the grace to accomplish, step by step, the journey that you desire each of us to make.

In reality, leaving behind our commitments to participate in a retreat calls for a breaking away which is costly. I found it even more difficult because, after a month's sojourn in Rome for the work of the Synod, many urgent tasks await me. I am therefore grateful to the Lord for giving me the strength to break away and come here, forgetting everything else. Of course, if we do not have the courage to allow others to complain a little about us, we will never be able to make an important decision.

Naturally, I am a bit awed by the experience of a retreat because, in fact, we are not capable of facing ourselves and God in truth. I am not able to express properly in words the journey of the Lord, nor do any of us manage to accept the way of true communion with him, with his Church, with the saints, with the kingdom. For this reason it is necessary to confess our impotence and to ask with humility for the gift of opening ourselves to the Holy Spirit.

The title of the retreat

I propose to reflect on Acts 20:18-38 where we find the 'pastoral testament' of Paul. The specific title of the retreat could be 'After some years' because in this text the apostle, speaking to the elders of Ephesus, stops to reconsider the human experience — presbyterial, pastoral, missionary — which he had lived for three years at Ephesus.

Sometimes we imagine that the discourse of Miletus, probably delivered in AD 58, is a synthesis of twenty or more years of ministry. It is certainly true that Paul had already completed about twenty years of his Christian journey, but no more than ten or twelve years of that was missionary experience which began around AD 46-47.

In Acts 20 he speaks only of what happened during the three years he spent in Ephesus. He is therefore reflecting on what we might call a medium term of presbyterial service. I would call short term that which takes place in a period in which we can verify our giving and receiving (meetings, colloquys, initiatives which are concluded over a period of a month or a year, summer day camps, the journey of a year with a youth group). Medium term is that which covers a period more complete in itself: two, three or four years.

It seems to me that Paul's reflection on his service at Ephesus can also help us to think about the moment where each of us finds himself some years after the beginning of ministry, so that we can verify the journey made and prepare new stages of the journey.

Suggestions

I would like to offer some suggestions in the hope that the retreat might become, above all, your own activity, a placing of yourself face-to-face with God, with yourself and with the Church, asking yourself: How do I see myself today? What do I think of myself? How do I understand myself? What do I find in my reality as a person, as a Christian, as a priest? What is my experience? What do I ask of you, Lord, what do I desire, what do I implore of your love?

My first suggestion is that each one of you should read Acts 20 in the light of the whole book. The discourse of Miletus, in fact, forms a whole with Paul's two preceding chapters — chapter 13, the kerygmatic one delivered to the Hebrews, and chapter 17, to the pagans.

The discourse of chapter 20 is addressed to the Church. It will be useful also to keep in mind the Second Letter to the Corinthians, the two Letters to Timothy and the Letter to Titus, because they echo strongly the themes covered by Paul in his discourse at Miletus.

Naturally, Dupont's *Il Testamento pastorale di San Paolo* could also be a help, but it requires a certain tranquillity to be understood and fully appreciated.

The second suggestion is to profit from these days by resting in silence and in tranquil prayer, almost letting time flow by without worrying about accomplishing anything.

The third is to commit ourselves to liturgical prayer, which will be carefully prepared.

The fourth suggestion is to establish certain periods for mental prayer. It would seem indispensable to have two half hours a day of real and proper mental prayer, to which it would be well to add a quarter of an hour of Eucharistic adoration. If we do not establish these moments with a certain discipline of spirit, and be quite concrete about them, we run the risk of never entering into reflective prayer.

Communication in faith

To me, the special importance of this retreat is being able to live a communion of faith with the bishop. I need it for my own personal, spiritual and pastoral journey; you also need it.

The communication will take place in four ways: firstly, praying together, because in this way we reach the roots of the person where, in Christ, we can communicate vitally, and secondly, writing down some reflections on your meditation.

We will also have communication in groups at determined hours. As you already know, this communication includes the desire to share with others, including the bishop, the consolations and intuitions which the Lord gives, and which have a communal character. It is also possible in group communication to ask questions and seek clarification of what we have heard in order to set up a dialogue of faith.

Finally, remember the means of communication provided by personal encounters, even though these are limited by the time at my disposal for meeting with you.

Our intercessors

I conclude by putting our retreat in the hands of Saint Charles. Incidentally, Charles Bascape, Borromeo's secretary, lived in this house and it was here that he prepared to write Borromeo's life. We also invoke Cardinal Ferrari and together with our archbishops we ask the intercession of Mary.

O Lord, who granted Saint Charles the grace to give himself body and soul for his flock, and who allowed him to enjoy in his pastoral service a profound interior joy and a great charity in its daily expression, we pray that you may allow us also to penetrate, by our contemplation of the crucified, into that fount of unity and light which we urgently need for our dispersed and fragmentary existence.

We pray, Lord Jesus, by the intercession of Blessed Cardinal Ferrari, that you may grant us strength of soul and true fatherhood through the strain of humiliations and solitude. Give us the grace to open our hearts to the maturity and growth of our humanity in the deepest sense of the mystery of humanity and of the mystery of your love for all humankind. Bring about in each of us a deep unity of life and of prayer.

O Lord, through the intercession of Mary, grant us the grace to live these days in communion with the universal Church of which Mary is mother. Help us to understand that we cannot do greater good to those we love and to those entrusted to us than by dedicating ourselves totally and courageously to prayer and silence during this retreat.

Mary, mother of Jesus and our mother, help us to be spiritually close to the whole world, to all the Churches whose bishops spoke the language of faith and the language of suffering and persecution at the Synod.

Obtain for us, to whom it is given to live these moments of peace and tranquillity, a courageous communion — an ascetical commitment — with those who, in the name of Christ, suffer hunger, solitude, prison, violence and the fear of death.

Do not allow us to remain in the background but, through a commitment to sacrifice and to a renunciation of fantasy in thought, in reading and in word, help us to place ourselves in harmony with the suffering Church which, throughout the world, gives witness to the cross of your son. Mary, grant that we may proclaim the glory of him who gives us the fullness of his Spirit and the grace of participating in his resurrection.

1

Confirmation and consolation

We want to begin this day, Lord, with the desire to listen to your words. Instil in our hearts the certainty that you speak to us, that your Spirit works in us with love and intelligence, that same Spirit which sustains and promotes the holy Church of believers in all the baptised and in those who are journeying towards the discovery or towards the maturity of faith. Enable us also to allow ourselves to be drawn by the light which shines from your side, crucified Lord, who died for us and who lives and reigns for ever and ever. Amen.

We are going to meditate on the whole discourse of Miletus; we will discuss its literary genre and, in particular, the two words which characterise the style and the scope of Paul's 'pastoral testament' — *confirmation* and *consolation*.

Let us therefore reflect on the general historical context in which these words were pronounced. We will then consider the more specific literary context of the passage; finally, we will consider briefly our own ecclesial context.

The general historical context
Paul, like the other apostles, generally concluded his apostolic missions with expressions of parenesis, that is exhortation, consolation and confirmation. When he took

leave of a community after a certain period of apostolic activity he delivered a discourse which he would take up again when circumstances brought him back to those same faithful.

Even at Miletus, therefore, he gives a *parenetic* discourse, different from a *kerygmatic* one (belonging to the first proclamation) and from a *didactic* discourse in which he explains truths and the duties of the Christian.

Before leaving Ephesus on the voyage to Macedonia, Paul had already addressed the community with similar expressions.

'After the uproar' — which occurred because of Artemide, described in chapter 19 — 'ceased, Paul sent for the disciples and having exhorted them took leave of them and departed for Macedonia' *(Acts 20:2)*. 'Exhortation' in Greek is *paraclesis* and literally signifies 'consolation'.

From Ephesus he arrives in Greece and meets again with some already evangelised communities. 'When he had gone through these parts and had given them much encouragement, he came to Greece' *(Acts 20:2)*.

Here too we are speaking of a discourse of consolation and in the Greek text the verb is the same as in verse 1: *parakalēsas autous* — having consoled them. In fact, they add *logō pollō* — with long discourses.

Paul usually abounded in expressions of consolation, perhaps more than necessary in the opinion of his listeners as is apparent in the same chapter 20 where the Apostle who must leave the next day 'prolonged [at Troade] his speech until midnight.... And a young man named Eutychus was sitting in the window. He sank into a deep sleep as Paul talked still longer and being overcome by sleep, he fell down from the third storey and was taken up

16

dead' *(7-9)*. Luke seems to insist on the length of the discourse and we can gather from this that the words of consolation were prolonged and ample.

A more detailed description of the visit and of Paul's leavetaking can be read in Acts 14.

'When they had preached the gospel to that city [Derbe] and had made many disciples, they returned to Lystra and to Iconium and to Antioch, strengthening the souls of the disciples, exhorting them to continue in the faith, and saying that through many tribulations we must enter the kingdom of God' *(21-22)*.

This is a second visit to a community evangelised earlier. A new verb is used here: 'reanimating them', in the Italian version. The Greek, more precisely, uses a circumlocution; *episterizontes tas psychas ton matheton,* fortifying souls, strengthening the psychology of the disciples.

To the more specific activity of consolation which we understand from chapter 20, we add that of strengthening, of confirming, of reinforcing them in their original commitment. We also have a synthesis of the contents of this sermon of consolation: '... through many tribulations we must enter the kingdom of God'. In fact, it is often the difficulties which block our journey of faith and dedication to the kingdom and here the apostle reminds them of the seriousness of the cross.

It is also interesting to read the narrative of Acts 15 where it is said that Paul and his companions went to Antioch to deliver to the community the letter of the Apostles and elders of the Church of Jerusalem: 'And when they read it, they rejoiced at the exhortation. And Judas and Silas, who were themselves prophets, exhorted the brethren with many words and strengthened them' *(31-32)*.

Acts 16 describes the aim of Paul's second pastoral visit,

17

which is to fortify and strengthen the community: Paul and Timothy, 'as they went on their way through the cities, ... delivered to them for observance the decisions which had been reached by the apostles and elders who were at Jerusalem. So the churches were strengthened in the faith...' *(4-5)*.

Here the verb used in the Greek text is *estereounto,* which has the same root as that which indicates strengthening and is also used in Acts 3 in regard to the cure of the cripple whose feet and ankles 'were made strong' *(7)*. The image is of one who walks badly, limping, risking a fall and who, at a certain point, is placed solidly on his feet. The communities visited by Timothy and Paul are therefore enabled to walk whereas before they were in constant danger of tripping and falling.

The same activity of the apostle is recalled in Acts 18, after his return from Antioch: 'After spending some time there he departed and went from place to place through the region of Galatia and Phrygia, strengthening all the disciples' *(23)*.

Here too we speak of reanimating, strengthening, building up the community and the life of the disciples.

From this first analysis we can conclude that the general historical context of the discourse of Miletus is one in which Paul, after the first evangelisation, either takes leave of a community or returns to visit them, aiming mainly at consolation and exhortation, at sustaining and strengthening the community.

The literary context
We must now consider the more specifically literary context of this discourse, one of the longest among Paul's many consolation discourses.

In its exterior configuration it contains words of farewell, of a definitive goodbye, and it is therefore also called 'the pastoral testament'. It is similar to the words of farewell and of final testament which Old Testament figures give before dying and expresses an attitude which is proper to all humanity. In fact, when a person is about to leave a place to which he has become attached, especially if he is close to dying, he instinctively wants to confide remembrances and last words to those who remain. Today our society has become much more reticent in these situations but in those families which continue the patriarchal traditions, it is still possible, for example, to encounter parents who, before dying, call their children around them to give their last recommendations, the last expressions of their heart.

I would like to recall here some of the better known scripture texts referring to this subject.

Genesis 49 gives us Jacob's discourse of farewell, his last words. Jacob calls his children together and to each expresses his affection and gives his benediction with a prediction, '... blessing each with a special blessing' *(28)*.

Deuteronomy is really conceived as Moses' long discourse of farewell and testament, especially chapters 1-4. Moses recalls in synthesis past events, expressing the desire that the people do not forget them. From chapters 31-33, we have the last actions of the prophet. Here, like a jewel in a fine setting, we have the famous 'Canticle', which was my inspiration for the pastoral letter, *God educates his people*. At a certain point it says: 'He found him in a desert land, and in the howling waste of the wilderness, he encircled him, he cared for him, he kept him as the apple of his eye' *(32:10)*.

In Joshua 23-24 we can read the testament pronounced

by Joshua in the great assembly gathered in Sichem.

In 1 Kings 20:1-9, David, now close to death, gives his last recommendations to his son Solomon.

Closer to Paul's discourse, even in content, are the words of Samuel when he says farewell to the people of Israel (1 Samuel 12:1-5), as also of Mattathias to his children (1 Mac 2:49-50). Father Dupont examines these at length in his work.

Here I would like to cite at least the words of Samuel: 'And Samuel said to all Israel, "Behold, I have hearkened to your voice in all that you have said to me and have made a king over you. And now, behold, the king walks before you; and I am old and grey, and behold, my sons are with you; and I have walked before you from my youth until this day. Here I am, testify against me before the Lord and before his anointed. Whose ox have I taken? Or whose ass have I taken? Or whom have I defrauded? Whom have I oppressed? Or from whose hand have I taken a bribe to blind my eyes with it? Testify against me and I will restore it to you." They said, "You have not defrauded us or oppressed us or taken anything from any man's hand." And he said to them, "The Lord is witness against you and his anointed is witness this day, that you have not found anything in my hand." And they said, "He is witness."'

Paul, in taking leave of the elders of Ephesus, also expresses his consciousness of having desired neither silver, nor gold nor the apparel of anyone (Acts 20:33-34).

Finally we can recall Tobit's last words to his son Tobias (Tob 14:3-11) and above all Jesus' great discourse of farewell to his disciples, according to the evangelist John (John 13-17).

Thus Paul's 'pastoral testament' is not an isolated case,

but can be set into the pattern of many discourses of farewell which, when studied attentively, cannot be taken only in their immediacy: Jacob, Samuel, David, Tobit — all pronounce words which enter into the activity of strengthening, comforting and consoling proper to those who have responsibility for others. By means of autobiographical reminiscences, a call to consider the past and protestations of his own honesty, the link between the apostle and the people is strengthened and the journey of the community confirmed.

It is clear that Paul's discourse at Miletus is valid for all the presbyters of the Church of every age and as such we must accept it.

The historical context

After trying to understand the historical context (words of consolation and exhortation at the end of a visit to the community after a certain period of pastoral activity) and the more precise literary context (the farewell discourse which, however, belongs to the genre of comfort and confirmation), we ask ourselves: Do we or do we not need words of consolation and strength?

From the *lectio*, or reflection on the passage and its contents, we thus pass to the *meditatio* or reflection on our own life experience and that of the Church.

First of all, let us see what sense the expressions of the apostle could have for the first Christian communities. Evidently, they suppose a situation of frailty in the faithful — frailty in the individual and frailty in the group. The Acts of the Apostles demonstrates with what ease the primitive Church broke into divisions, each setting itself against another. So much suffering, bitterness and tension was born from that fragile communion of hearts. The

Christians lived admirable and extraordinary moments in their experience of faith which, nonetheless, did not last long; there was a constant need to restrengthen communion. Let us think then of the frailty brought about by the community's being immersed in a pagan world — frivolous, consumerist, pleasure-seeking, indifferent, open to all cults but not ready to listen to any of them. It should not surprise us if the faithful let themselves be discouraged, tempted by the desire to leave and to go back on their promises, and by hypocrisy (Anania and Saphira, see Acts 5:1-11).

What about us? Here in the present generation the theme of frailty arises with ever-greater frequency. It is said that adolescents, young people, even young priests are good and generous, but they do not hold out for long, they tire easily and need to be continually sustained.

The first reflection, coming from Paul's words at Miletus is that even the first Christians were fragile; we are not, therefore, living in a new condition. If this were not true, the apostle would not have needed to visit them once again to bring them consolation and comfort. Therefore, we can frankly admit our frailty without being ashamed of it.

The second reflection is that we should not be surprised by frailty and not seek a scapegoat. Let us not be surprised if our young people, after a few months of good will, are stopped by the first difficulty they encounter and end up by dissolving a group. Let us not wonder if young couples fight over nothing and are tempted by the idea of separation. Human frailty must be taken seriously.

The third reflection comes as a consequence. Given the reality of this frailty, it cannot be enough to stir up the first commitment.

Taking Paul's example, we must continually reanimate

adolescents, young couples, politicians who start out well and then tire, letting themselves be overcome by the heavy atmosphere and the prevailing corruption. We must reanimate the workers who have created a group of pastoral workers and have then lost faith in it. We must reanimate the youth who begin to visit the old and the handicapped and after a short time can no longer remember the motivation for their commitment.

Our people, our communities must be reanimated constantly; we too must allow ourselves to be reanimated because the enthusiasm of our ordination or the joy of a few moments of spiritual retreat are not enough. Let us therefore learn from St Paul to mature day after day in the knowledge of human frailty.

By means of continuous confirmation, consolation, strengthening and comfort, we can grow without pretending to hasten the times of the psychological and biological process but respecting the seasons, remembering that our fathers in the faith and the apostles made the same journey and were not frightened by the gradual steps which make up life.

I invite you in your personal meditation to reread the Pauline passages to clarify the confirmation which each of us needs, to reflect on the specific frailty which has emerged in these first years of presbyterial experience. It will probably be a frailty which did not manifest itself in the seminary due to the support structure which, in a certain sense, protected you.

We can also dare to ask the question which corresponds to the biblical words: 'What consolations do I need?' — consolations regarding affection, feelings, emotions, sadness, bitterness, solitude, anger, conflicts in which we are caught up and which often need the oil of consolation, the balm of the Spirit, the interior dew which comes from above.

I believe it is important during this first morning of the retreat to take time to write the answer to these two questions:

> What confirmation do I need above all, Lord, both from you and from others — from the community, from the bishop, from my brothers?
>
> What words of consolation do I most lack?

Freeing ourselves before God in sincerity, we will better understand the consoling power of the Church, we will open ourselves to receive it, to ask for it when we need it for the growth of our faith and love.

May the Lord help us, therefore, to open ourselves to the action of the Paraclete Spirit who comes forth from his wounded heart and may he remind us that the ministry confided in Peter and communicated to all the Church is a service of confirmation and of strengthening.

2

Frailty Strengthened

The icon we might keep before us is Jesus' encounter with the two disciples of Emmaus (Luke 24:13-35).

Jesus, you know that I am in need of confirmation, comfort, encouragement and consolation. Help me to allow myself to be comforted by you so that, in turn, I may comfort and console others. You patiently listened, healed, reanimated and brought new warmth to the hearts of the two disciples of Emmaus; teach us to contemplate you at length, in prayer and adoration, that we may be able to participate in your ministry of being a good shepherd.

If we look at our great models — St Charles Borromeo and Blessed Cardinal Ferrari — we realise that a good part of their preaching was parenetic, exhortative, consoling and confirming. However, we also need personal encouragement and comfort.

Therefore, I would like to prolong the reflection on the parenetic characteristic of our pastoral action and to draw forth all the wealth it contains. We might call this meditation: 'Frailty strengthened, sadness consoled, weakness healed'. Thus we explain the belief that frailty exists, sadness arises, weakness is manifested but that there is strengthening, consolation and healing. It is there for us who, as pastors, must learn more and more to heal and confirm.

First, let us ask ourselves what the daily frailties are. Then we will seek the remedies the Lord gives for strengthening ourselves and our brothers and sisters.

The weakness of the contemporary world
Let us start with the frailty and incoherence of the young people that we know, those to whom we have listened in confession or who have confided their problems to us. As we consider these young people, we must bear in mind that each of us passes through the same trials of faith and of hope that our contemporaries are living.

It is a common occurrence in the 1980s to repeat that the present generation is different from that of the 1960s and the beginning of the 1970s when arrogance and disrespect emerged. Today we note a greater capacity to listen even in quite secularised milieux; people want to learn and, on the whole, are not arrogant. All the same, they reveal strange inconsistencies as unexpected as they are unforeseen — which surprise those affected by them: Why and how did I arrive at this point? Why do I no longer have the desire to follow the way or the commitment chosen?

It seems useful, therefore, to reflect on the possible reasons for our inconsistencies which are at the root of small, and sometimes large, inexplicable actual surrenders. Evidently we are not very different from our predecessors, but the phenomenon of frailty, at least in the West, is too generalised not to have common causes.

1. The first of these causes is that we live in an epoch

of profound social change. Ideas, customs, ways of thinking, attitudes and ideologies all change rapidly. This produces a sense of bewilderment because it does not allow us to anchor ourselves to habits or to precise points of reference. It is then a factor which we must take into account. Examining history, we realise that this is not really anything new: the passage of Israel from a nomadic to a settled people, from a state of possession to exile, from exile to the restoration and then to the Roman invasion was certainly marked by important cultural changes — again, the times of the barbarian invasions were characterised by a profound social mutation. However, it is probable that today we are present at a unique period of rapid change, which influences the stability and the constancy of the personality.

2. A second cause, which is similar to the first and represents its cultural projection, is diffused pluralism. In our pluralistic society each person thinks and expresses himself as he desires; we can have all the information we want from the newspapers, we are made aware of many ideologies. Thus it is more difficult to orient oneself today than it was in a primitive, agricultural society where one idea prevailed. Today, any single or unique idea is questioned.

3. Consumerism is a third reason which explains why frailty is above all a characteristic of the West. People are worn down by the many material goods which condition them and which — at least in the beginning — bring licit satisfaction. We continually seek small and large stimulation: we cannot do without television, without our soft drinks or coffee at a snack bar, without the latest novelty

in food, or in home furnishings, or in clothes. A thriftier and more austere society evidently cultivated a great capacity for interior fortitude.

4. The mass media multiply the effects of social change, of pluralism and of consumerism because they propagate them and cause them to penetrate the quiet of our homes. At any given moment we can be caught up by consumerism and by the multiplicity of prevailing opinions.

All these are motives to keep in mind. Each demands a remedy, a discipline, and calls for a certain type of pastoral care to help the faithful. However, they ask first of all for a serious exercise of asceticism on our part.

5. There is, none the less, a frailty which is perhaps even more typical of contemporary consciousness and of the modern and post-modern Western civilisation. It is so subtle and rich in values that we have difficulty in analysing it in depth. I want to speak of the cancerous growth of subjectivity, that is, that world which is called forth by words and phrases such as 'person', 'consciousness', 'interiority', 'personal conviction', 'authenticity', 'spontaneity', 'personal sensitivity', 'respect for one's own feelings'.

These are a series of important values that were already present in ancient times, since the time of Socrates, but they have never been so popular as they are today. We have acquired an awareness of our own subjectivity. Consider, for example, the discussions aroused about the teaching of religion, and the power a minority has when, however small its number, it manages nonetheless to touch the chords of contemporary consciousness. Consider the discussions of the liberty of the child, equal rights, non-discrimination, etc.

We need to ask the Lord for enlightened discernment because we are faced with a reality rich in values which, in the classical tradition, has its origins in Socrates, in Plato, in Neoplatonism, in that introspection developed by the philosophers; in the Christian journey this reality has its model above all in scripture. The centrality of humankind, of the person, of consciousness, of the heart, is repeatedly underlined in the New Testament and later developed by means of positive and specific reflections on interiority beginning with Augustine, one of the great Fathers of the West. These values are important, and must be taken seriously into account in our pastoral service: the sense of interior liberty, respect for each person, consciousness, attention to coherence between thought and feeling, thought and action, authenticity, spontaneity. We ourselves have to struggle to fit into already existing patterns, to obey fully institutions or traditions passed on to us, when these do not seem to flow forth immediately from the depths of our consciousness.

In my opinion, it is necessary first of all to live an attentive gratitude to God for the fundamental value of interiority.

'I thank you, Lord, because you have revealed my heart to me, because you have revealed the value of the interior person, because in the words of Augustine you told me that *in interiore homine habitat veritas* (truth lives within a man) and through Jesus you said, ''Blessed are the pure of heart for they shall see God.'' '

In this way it will be easier for us to discover the counterfeits of interiority, the cancerous growth of subjective consciousness which goes beyond what is right, times of abnormal and pretentious development. All the same, we are not always able to distinguish true values from

29

their counterfeits, which can fool even those who want to live the so-called spiritual life. They are the typical temptations of the scribes and pharisees, of all of us who seek to refine ourselves intellectually and to strive for some important values.

I believe we can speak of the cancerous growth of subjectivity when consciousness (personal or group, because this is also a defect of groups) tends, for example, to become solipsistic, setting itself up as the sole measure of its own actions. The most frequent form of such an aberration occurs when the monologue between the individual and his own feelings acquires the value of a 'diktat', of a norm that cannot be disregarded, of desires which cannot be questioned. Thus, in reality, the only coherence sought is with one's own feelings, one's own emotions. The results, disconcerting in their apparent innocence, are expressed in relation to commitments taken and promises made in the following terms: 'I don't feel up to it anymore.' 'Faith, the Church, the celebration of Mass, no longer mean anything to me!' 'I have cut myself off from that person because they no longer mean anything to me.'

We must note that all this is mistaken for an authentic desire. The flowering of interior feelings, without contextual comparisons with surrounding influences and values, becomes the legitimate and definitive norm: 'I have lived with my wife (with my husband) for ten wonderful years, but now she (he) no longer has relevance for my life, now our acts are no longer spontaneous'. These simple attitudes, apparent legitimations, are the cancerous growth of the supremacy of individual consciousness.

When we speak of the consciousness of a group, this growth is more harmful and more disastrous. We can call to mind, for example, groups of terrorists for whom certain ways of thinking and acting were considered right until at a certain point they declared that they had changed their minds and that this period was over.

Here we find ourselves at the heart of one of the roots of contemporary frailty. If we were to examine the different crises of the family, the actual crises of priests and religious, we would find that at the heart of it all is the 'supreme norm' of one's own feelings.

I must emphasise here that to live in this way is extremely difficult because the supremacy of conscience, which is objective and founded on the truth of the presence of the Holy Spirit in each of us, is confused with the continuous overflowing of our feelings and emotions. All of this ends by upsetting our psychological equilibrium and thus the need arises for tranquilisers, psychological counselling and the like.

It is a life in which people, convinced that they are finding themselves, lose themselves. According to the words of Christ: 'He who seeks his life, will lose it' *(Luke 17:33)*.

The ministry of consolation

We are children of our times and, one day, we may find ourselves suddenly hypnotised by the upsurge of a subjectivity which commands, preventing us from achieving or even working towards goals that we had set.

For this reason also, it is important to be aware of the remedies the Holy Spirit puts at our disposal to console us and to console others, to confirm us and to confirm others, to heal us and to heal others.

1. The Holy Spirit is the real Paraclete, the perfect consoler of humankind. John Paul II has written splendidly in his encyclical on the Holy Spirit, *Dominum et Vivificantem,*

on the office of confirming and of reinforcing which belongs especially to the Holy Spirit. I advise you to reread those pages in both the second part of the encyclical — where he explains how the Holy Spirit convicts us of sin and places us before the cross of Christ — and the third part, nn. 58 and 59. By ourselves we are not capable of keeping a proper focus on our own interiority; we must continue to rediscover it in the light of grace. The Spirit is given to us by God in his mercy to free us from our superficiality, from our frivolity and escapism, from our false interiority, in order to restore to us the true and full concept of ourselves. 'Thanks to the divine communication the human spirit... encounters the "Spirit who scrutinises the depths of God". In this Spirit who is eternal gift, God one and three opens himself to us, to the human spirit.'

I suggest that for your personal meditation you place yourself in adoration and prayer before this Spirit, perhaps repeating slowly the sequence 'Come, Holy Spirit', which develops the fundamental theme: the Spirit who consoles, comforts and confirms, who strengthens the inner person.

The first remedy is, therefore, not to presume that we can do it alone but to implore the Holy Spirit to fill our hearts, to light in us the fire of his love, to warm our coldness and to give light to our minds.

2. The consoling action of the Spirit demonstrates the supernatural meaning of the journey of the cross. This is the way in which God consoles, this is the word of Jesus to the disciples of Emmaus: 'O foolish men and slow of heart to believe all that the prophets have spoken! Was it not necessary that the Christ should suffer these things and enter into his glory?' *(Luke 24:25-26)*. The explanation of the journey of the cross through the use of scripture makes

the disciples' hearts burn with love and therefore consoles, confirms, gives new meaning to life and to sacrifice, demonstrating the balance between the journey to regain our own liberty and the goal of glory and resurrection.

The supernatural meaning of the cross is expressed by St Paul in the passage mentioned above, where he reanimates and exhorts the disciples to remain firm in faith because 'through many tribulations we must enter the kingdom of God' *(Acts 14:22)*.

3. Finally, we can save ourselves from an exasperated subjectivity by abandoning ourselves to the words and gestures of the Church without always asking ourselves what meaning or relevance they have for us. At times there is a sort of anxiety about wanting to know the why or the wherefore of every single liturgical gesture or institutional reality, an anxiety which indicates the will to find always and everywhere a justification at the level of feeling.

Sometimes an exaggerated subjectivity even marks the experience of prayer. It is not true that insistently requesting God to 'teach me to pray' can hide the desire to taste our dialogue with the Lord sensibly and so verify it immediately. This gives rise to a search for a prayer which satisfies us and to a rejection of situations which do not allow us to have a discerning verification.

Here we are face-to-face with a spiritual illness which afflicts everyone in some way. It will probably take our whole lives to complete the journey of purification described by St John of the Cross and St Teresa of Avila which would have us pass from a sensible and emotive immediacy to greater and better founded objectivity.

The Church with its liturgy, with its gestures and words, is a guarantee of objectivity which helps us to enter into the truth of prayer and into the nakedness of faith.

Grant us, Mary, to comfort the many afflictions which we encounter on our journey, and that we often cannot heal with mere human words. Help us to comfort the many physical ills of the people who continually come before us, and even more, the bitter and secret interior afflictions which burden the journey of so many men, women, young adults and adolescents. At times their sufferings are not expressed but even so they await a word of comfort from us, a gesture which is a sign of the consoling action of the Holy Spirit.

Lord, by the intercession of Mary, open our hearts above all to the merciful action of the Spirit, to the beneficial power of holy scripture, the Gospel, and to the comforting words and gestures of the Church.

3

The Call to the Banquet

Homily for the Mass of Tuesday, 31st Week of the Year

Let us ask God the Father to grant us a deeper understanding of the centrality of the Eucharistic liturgy in our lives and prayer together during these days of retreat.

In fact, it is the Eucharist of the diocese, celebrated by the bishop with some priests, that represent the whole presbytery: here we see expressed in a privileged way the local Church's consciousness of being called to unity by the Word, for the sacramental union with the body of Christ who offers himself for humanity.

But the Eucharist also constructs the city of humankind. In this sense, I recall the fine words of Father Joseph Dossetti, on 1 October last at the Eucharistic Congress of Bologna. After asking what the significance of the city is and what the ambiguities of its values are today, Father Dossetti demonstrated how the Eucharist is the moment at which the Christian contributes most to the building of this city, thanks to the faith, hope and charity connected with and coming from participation in the sacramental celebration. May the Lord make us more deeply aware, at the level of interiority, of this fundamental reality.

Romans 12:5-16

The first reading is a typical example of parenesis, of Pauline exhortation:

'... so we, though many, are one body in Christ and individually members one of another. Having gifts that differ according to the grace given to us, let us use them: if prophecy, in proportion to our faith; if service, in our serving; he who teaches, in his teaching; he who exhorts, in his exhortation; he who contributes, in liberality; he who gives aid, with zeal; he who does acts of mercy, with cheerfulness.

'Let love be genuine; hate what is evil, hold fast to what is good; love one another with brotherly affection; outdo one another in showing honour. Never flag in zeal, be aglow with the Spirit, serve the Lord. Rejoice in your hope, be patient in tribulation, be constant in prayer. Contribute to the needs of the saints, practise hospitality. Bless those who persecute you; bless and do not curse them. Rejoice with those who rejoice, weep with those who weep. Live in harmony with one another; do not be haughty but associate with the lowly; never be conceited.'

When we speak of long exhortations in Acts, expressions of this type come to mind, appearing like arrows or darts, not like moralistic assertions. The community is shaken up and, under the effect of this sting, hidden energies are set in motion.

The tone of this passage reminds us of the First Letter to the Corinthians where Paul describes the charisms, the ministries, the services through which each expresses his subjectivity and where there is then a very forceful call to live that charity which takes account of the whole body (1 Corinthians 12-13).

In the Letter to the Romans, the progression is more

tranquil. Paul starts with the different gifts that should be exercised according to the particular laws proper to each charism and then describes the charity which embraces everything globally: 'Hate what is evil, hold fast to what is good, love one another... bless those who persecute you. Do not be haughty....' We can recognise here the characteristics of the hymn of love in 1 Corinthians 13: 'Love does not insist on its own way... [love] believes all things, hopes all things, endures all things.'

Charity is not considered a specific virtue alongside the others, rather it is a charism which concerns the global nature of the body of the Church, one that must inspire all actions and all individual services.

I leave it to you to reflect on the condition of the priest who, as the one responsible for the community, stands on the side of the whole, and thus of charity. The priest must get a capacity for distinguishing the sectional from the whole, and so not fall into the confusion of being satisfied with the generosity or the enthusiasm of some single service which may perhaps be to the detriment of the whole.

Luke 14:15-24

This is a passage from what is called the 'convivial' chapter because everything happens during banquets. At the beginning there is the healing of a crippled man during a banquet; then, beginning with verse 7, general indications for the invitation to a wedding feast or a supper are given. Finally, there is the parable of the great call which, in the tradition of the Church, reaches its deepest significance in the Eucharist.

'When one of those who sat at table with him heard this he said to him: "Blessed is he who shall eat bread in the kingdom of God!" But he said to him, "A man once gave a great banquet and invited many; and at the time for the banquet he sent his servant to say to those who had been invited, 'Come, for all is now ready'. But they all alike began to make excuses. The first said to him 'I have bought a field and I must go out and see it; I pray you, have me excused.' And another said 'I have bought a yoke of oxen and I have to go examine them; I pray you have me excused.' And another said, 'I have married a wife and therefore I cannot come.' So the servant came and reported this to his master. Then the householder in anger said to his servant: 'Go out quickly to the streets and lanes of the city, and bring in the poor and maimed and blind and lame.' And the servant said: 'Sir, what you command has been done and there is room still.' And the master said to the servant, 'Go out to the highways and hedges and compel people to come in that my house may be filled. For I tell you, none of those who were invited shall taste my banquet.' " ' "

Let me stress that the legitimisations of subjectivity brought into focus by the parable are tied up with human frailty. We find people who excuse themselves for undeniably good reasons: the field needs special attention; the five pair of oxen represent a capital which cannot be ignored; a wife has her rightful needs.

All the same, the paradoxical insistence of the parable brings to light the fact that over-inflated subjectivity closes its eyes to the reality of what makes us persons. Neither the field nor the oxen nor even a spouse makes me a person if I am not open to the invitation of the Lord.

Things that are temporal, subjective, secular — to use the language of the Synod — can hide what really counts, that is, the call.

One can thus understand why some synodal fathers were

quite obstinate in amending again and again the proposals of those who wanted to define the Christian lay person as one who is essentially related to the secular, as if a relationship with temporal things as such were capable of defining the value of the person.

The gospel warns us about the ambiguities of secularity represented by the field, the oxen, the wife. The relations which take place in the temporal sphere certainly have a positive significance but they can blind us to the divine call which, when accepted, puts the field, the oxen and all the rest in their correct place.

Here a fundamental defect of human consciousness is stressed — that of considering ourselves constituted by our choice and not by our call. It is a risk which follows us continually and is so linked to our frailty as to merit attentive reflection.

In Jesus' parable, the poor accept the invitation. They are those who have preserved the sense of their own relativity as persons; they know that they are not the epicentre to which all must be referred. They accept being relative to the realities constituted by the richness of the banquet. The poor, therefore, are available to the call because they are aware of not having in themselves the ultimate reason for their choices. This marvellous emphasis is one of the constants of the gospel and it should make us thoughtful and circumspect also about the way we look at ourselves and organise our lives. Our sadness, our uncertainty, our weakness, all have one of their fundamental roots here.

The poor, however, are blessed because they refer to things greater than themselves. At times, looking at our restored cathedral and thinking of the expense of making it even more splendid, I ask myself: Was it really necessary?

Couldn't we sell all the treasures here and give the money to the poor?

However, reflecting on the generations who found in the symbol of the temple a sense of their own relativity to a reality greater than themselves, it seems necessary to respond that even the restoration of a cathedral, of a church, is indeed a service to the poor, to the hundreds of millions of persons who are comforted, sustained and cheered by these symbols which refer us to other things.

Maybe it is for this reason that those who have less are more prepared to give towards the construction or restoration of a temple.

While visiting the native populations of Africa and Latin America I could see their capacity for rejoicing in their participation in communal undertakings, because they understand that great collective symbols are a richness and lead us to what can fill us permanently, like the great parable of the banquet.

Lord, grant us the grace to understand the importance of the truth to which we are dedicated, and help us to overcome hasty and vague subjectivity (even when it appears as charisms) so that we may achieve a sense of wholeness.

This is the grace that we ask in this Eucharist for each of us, for our Church and for all the Churches in communion with Rome.

4

Tears and Pastoral Trials

*Lord, you gave St Charles Borromeo the grace to be a good
shepherd for your people and you made him into an image of
you — the Good Shepherd — for all succeeding generations
up to the present. You filled him with the endless depths of
your love for humanity so that his works sometimes appear
incapable of our imitation.*

*O Jesus, on the occasion of this liturgical feast we ask that
as Elisha received a third of the prophetic spirit of Elijah, we
may be gifted with at least part of the pastoral spirit of St
Charles, so that we may be sustained in the trials of our
ministry, enumerated by Paul as a distinctive sign of his mission
in Asia.*

Today we will reflect on the first part of the discourse
of Miletus where the apostle recalls the three years lived
at Ephesus. However, I would like to begin by recalling
four moments of the exercise of the *lectio divina* since our
meditations follow this method. They are the moments of
lectio, meditatio, contemplatio and *consolatio.*

The work of the *lectio* is to deepen our knowledge of the
text through re-reading it, emphasising its main elements,
comparing them with the remote as well as with the more
immediate context.

The *lectio* flows into the *meditatio*. Here the aim is to reflect on the values and on the permanent message of the passage, to understand what it says to each one of us, to the Church and to the world today.

Obviously, the *meditatio* must not close itself into a certain damaging subjectivity but rather become a step towards the *contemplatio* which is the more prayerful moment. I place myself before him who speaks to me through the word of scripture, that is, before the Lord Jesus, the Incarnate Word. In the *contemplatio* we are enabled to open ourselves to grace, to throw our hearts open to the divine will.

Finally, the *consolatio*. We have already mentioned the importance of consolation for the Christian community and for ourselves. It is also the fruit of apostolic parenesis, that is the consoling and confirming discourse. Never the less, the principal place where the Spirit allows us to taste him as interior nourishment, as dew, balsam, oil and perfume, is the contemplation for which we prepare ourselves by means of our journey into the *lectio*. We must be aware of this in order not to invoke the gift of consolation vainly when we feel the need to receive it either in the immediate form of joy, peace and serenity, in feeling that we are in love with God or in a deeper form which has less to do with feelings, but is, however, more authentic and profound because in this case there is no danger of confusing the gift with purely human sentiments.

As I noted in the introduction, the retreat has a value above all for the journey of *lectio* that each of you accomplishes, a journey that I am trying to set in motion. Evidently it is a work which does not limit itself rigorously to the moment of meditation but little by little permeates one's whole day, bringing unity between different actions.

In fact, the taste for God, so important for sustaining

the pastor in his solitude, can be given even at other moments to those who live the *lectio,* for example, during the liturgy or when we walk in the garden reciting a decade of the rosary. What I want to emphasise is that the *lectio divina* is the ordinary means of arriving at that mysterious embrace of the Holy Spirit, at that sign of the gift which God diffuses in our hearts by means of the Spirit who has been given us.

Subdivisions of the discourse of Miletus

We read in Acts 20:17-38: 'And from Miletus he sent to Ephesus and called to him the elders of the Church. And when they came to him he said to them:

"You yourselves know how I lived among you all the time from the first day that I set foot in Asia, serving the Lord with all humility and with tears and with trials which befell me through the plots of the Jews; how I did not shrink from declaring to you anything that was profitable, and teaching you in public and from house to house, testifying both to Jews and to Greeks of repentance to God and of faith in our Lord Jesus Christ. And now, behold, I am going to Jerusalem, bound in the Spirit, not knowing what shall befall me there; except that the Holy Spirit testifies to me in every city that imprisonment and afflictions await me. But I do not account my life of any value nor as precious to myself, if only I may accomplish my course and the ministry which I received from the Lord Jesus, to testify to the gospel of the grace of God. And now, behold, I know that all you among whom I have gone about preaching the kingdom will see my face no more. Therefore I testify to you this day that I am innocent of the blood of all of you, for I did not shrink from declaring to you the whole counsel of God. Take heed to yourselves and to all the flock, in which the Holy Spirit has made you guardians, to feed the Church of the Lord which he obtained with his own blood. I know that after my departure fierce wolves will come in among you, not sparing the flock; and from among your own selves will arise men speaking perverse things to draw away the disciples after them. Therefore, be alert, remembering that for three years I did not cease night or day to admonish every one with tears. And now I commend you to God and to the word of his grace, which is able to build you up and to give you the inheritance among all those who are sanctified. I coveted no one's silver or gold or apparel. You yourselves know that these hands ministered to my necessities and to those who were with me. In all things I have shown you that by so toiling one must help the weak, remembering the words of the Lord Jesus, how he said, 'It is more blessed to give than to receive.'

And when he had spoken thus, he knelt down and prayed with them all. And they all wept and embraced Paul and kissed him, sorrowing most of all because of the words he had spoken, that they should see his face no more. And they brought him to the ship.'

To do a *lectio* of such a long biblical passage it is necessary to divide it into its parts. The operation is obvious but not always easy. In fact, this discourse is subdivided in different ways by the exegetes precisely because it is dense and made up of parts. It is already important to understand that it is born of Paul's strong emotions and, therefore, that pastoral life is the source of intense and complex sentiments.

Fundamentally, we can distinguish three parts in the discourse:

—remembrance (vv 18-21), where Paul recalls his ministry in Asia;

—consciousness (vv 22-27), where he expresses his knowledge of the present and of what awaits him;
—commitment (vv 28-31), or the parenesis to the presbyters.

There follows the conclusion (vv 32-35), in which Paul synthesises some ideas presented earlier, and a final narrative (vv 36-38) which takes up the theme of tears and prayer again. I want to emphasise how the triple division can constitute a pastoral reflection that is to be transformed into prayer.

'Lord, help me to remember the ministry experienced in these past years, the joyful and painful experiences that you gave me, enabling the truly important realities to emerge in me through a remembrance that is reasonable and just, not guilt-ridden but grateful and appreciative.'

'Lord, let me be conscious of my present, that I may be aware of my relationship with you when I evaluate the past and when I come face-to-face with the task which awaits me.'

'Lord, help me·to translate into practical commitments the consequences of this remembrance and this consciousness.'

Beginning the *lectio*
The first part of the discourse of Miletus which we have called remembrance includes in the Italian translation two long sentences, both introduced with 'You know'. From Miletus Paul has the elders of the Church called to Ephesus and when they arrive he says: 'You yourselves know how I lived among you all the time from the first day that I set foot in Asia, serving the Lord with all humility and with tears and with trials which came before me through the plots of the Jews, [you know] how I did not shrink from declaring to you anything that was profitable, and teaching

45

you in public and from house to house, testifying both to Jews and to Greeks of repentance to God and of faith in our Lord Jesus Christ' *(18-21)*.

The remembrance of the apostle thus aims to involve the presbyters, calling them to give witness to him. It is an example, perhaps a rare one, of the leader of a community involving all the others, of indicating that the journey was made publicly, with them and among them. Paul's subjectivity is expressed in the institutional dimension of the Church and includes the presbyters and the faithful.

What do the elders of Ephesus know of Paul? Here I suggest that we put order into the elements that he brings forth out of his remembrance, keeping in mind that at the beginning the work of *lectio* is also analytical. From the ministry lived in Asia Paul recalls:

—the exterior circumstances, i.e. the facts that brought about the tears, and the trials caused by the plots laid by the Jews;

—the typically missionary and pastoral actions. A central action — 'I served the Lord' — and then preaching, teaching and beseeching;

—the interior attitudes which are two — 'In all humility', and without shrinking from what could be useful to the community, that is, courageously;

—the end for which Paul struggled — conversion to God and adherence to faith in the Lord Jesus.

Thus the apostle remembers his mission in Asia, expressing himself in few words, but words dense in meaning, affirmation and passionate feeling. Naturally I

46

will limit myself to bringing out only a few aspects of Paul's message, inviting you to continue personally the *lectio* and the *meditatio* of the passage. In teaching the *lectio divina*, in fact, it is necessary to indicate grains, seeds of mustard or pepper, so that they may be ground up and introduced into the global reflection.

The remembrance of the circumstances

The exterior circumstances of the Pauline ministry in Asia are tears and trials. It is certainly not a pleasant or attractive image of apostolic action and seems rather provocative when compared with some of Paul's other writings which begin with expressions of joy and satisfaction.

On the other hand, he is not speaking with bitterness here; he considers it proper to emphasise these circumstances of suffering rather than others and he indicates that they are characteristic of serving the Lord.

1. Let us reflect first of all on tears. The theme is not familiar to us but our Milan saints, Ambrose and Charles, knew it well and often spoke about it. In the discourse of Miletus it occurs again in verse 31: 'Therefore be alert, remembering that for three years I did not cease night or day to admonish every one with tears.'

Thus it seems that Paul considers this characteristic important. Tears are recalled at other times in his letters. In 2 Corinthians 2:2, for example, he mentions a previous letter written 'out of much affliction and anguish of heart and with many tears...'. In Philippians 3:18 he mentions breaking into tears in his ministry: 'For many of whom I have often told you and now tell you even with tears live as enemies of the cross of Christ'.

Therefore it can be useful to ask ourselves: Why does

Paul attach so much importance to tears? What do they signify? Certainly they are the opposite of that pastoral joy which is the fundamental attitude of the presbyter, of the bishop; as is stated in 1 Thessalonians: 'For what thanksgiving can we render to God for you, for all the joy which we feel for your sake before our God...?' *(3:9)*

A pastor knows what a great joy it is to see a community go forward, well-ordered and filled with faith; how great a joy it is to find a lost lamb or to go to meet a prodigal son as he returns home.

Tears express suffering for a community that does not go forward, that is struggling; the pain over those who have drifted away; the anxiety for those who are getting lost; the fear for those who began with enthusiasm and then stopped. There are many occasions of pastoral suffering and even if tears are not always visible, in our hearts uneasiness, strain and anguish are to be found.

The greater our responsibility for others and the more it is complete and lived with love, the more intense will be the joy and the pain. Only a pastor can rejoice when the flock goes well and cry when the wolf comes, because he who is not a pastor is a mercenary and does not have real love for the sheep (John 10). The mercenary has the characteristics of a bureaucrat who does everything possible not to get involved and to defend himself.

Why does Paul speak like this of tears? Why does Luke put into Paul's mouth these unfashionable characteristics? It seems to me that in the discourse of Miletus tears are mentioned because they prove above all the passion of service — tenderness, affection, participation and involvement.

With one word Paul expresses the world of affectivity that he has created between himself and his people in a brief few years, a world of relationships which are profound, friendly, true and decisive.

I would like to suggest three conclusions which can help us to pass from the *lectio* to the *meditatio*.

i)   It is not wrong or strange to experience pastoral suffering. The care of others, above all in the development of their liberty, implies the risk of refusal. Whenever there is refusal the pastor should suffer not because he has failed but because there was no response to God.

Tears do not express the pastor's bitterness at his lack of success; rather they indicate his affection for the persons who were given to him and who have not understood the invitation of the Lord. It is pain for the love of God which was not accepted.

ii)   Less laments, more tears; less complaints, more tears, we could say. In my pastoral visits it often happens that I hear the laments of those in charge: the young people don't come to church, they don't show up after they receive Confirmation, families don't get involved.

All the same, I have the impression that these complaints have nothing to do with tears. They are often said with irritation and disappointment and thus turn out to be sterile. Often enough, the tone of our complaints is self-accusatory or accuses others — those who are insensitive, or who are ignorant.

We must cry above all because they do not respond to God, because love is not loved, because God, infinite Love, is not loved as he should be. These tears are evangelical, creative, purifying. They melt personal bitterness and the offences that touch us. They let us take the situation in hand once more.

In the writings of Paul, we never find useless recriminations. Instead we find reproaches that are affectionate, trusting and encouraging. Perhaps in remembering his tears at Ephesus we can find the key to asking ourselves what makes us suffer and what makes us rejoice in our pastoral action, to reflect on the way in which we love the Lord and our brothers and sisters, to verify whether or not we suffer for the lack of response to God and rejoice when the response is given, whether we weep or whether we lament uselessly.

iii) We cannot say whether or not Paul's tears are for his own sins also. Certainly, however, St Ambrose and St Charles cried for their sins, and I think Blessed Cardinal Ferrari did likewise.

These tears are also creative because they are a sign of contrition for the laziness, the slowness, the weakness with which we live our pastoral ministry. Sincere repentance is born and turns into prayer: 'Forgive me Lord, have pity on me, a sinner, help me and save me!' Each of you could prolong this prayer in meditation and adoration.

2. The second exterior circumstance mentioned by Paul is trials. During the three years lived in Ephesus, Paul found people who were against him, who laid snares for him in various ways, degrading him and criticising him.

I read, in these circumstances, the admonition not to be surprised if we encounter in our ministry those who oppose us, who sow calumnies, who write anonymous letters.

Trials are not necessarily a negative sign, because Jesus himself lived them before Paul did. The experience remembered by the apostle warns us, however, not to confuse trials with plots. 'I served the Lord ... among trials which befell me through the plots of the Jews.' These latter are evil, detestable and wicked; Paul resisted them because he was able to distinguish between the action of the person (which could arouse in him indignation, anger, disgust, revenge) and the presence of the Lord which put him to the test on the way of the cross, which he viewed with trepidation and love.

The grace of seeing the hand of God which used human deception permitted Paul to put things into perspective, and so to live at liberty and with a certain tranquillity of soul, without being overcome.

I could relate many cases in which the malignity of the people ended up by bringing the one affected by it first to rebellion and then to desperation; others, on the contrary, who accepted these deceptions in the light of the trials of the Lord, grew in maturity and were happy to share in the agony of Christ, of the cross.

'Grant us, Lord, by the intercession of Paul to be able to make this important discernment when we find ourselves undergoing trials. Help us to understand that you have foreseen everything to enable us to travel — contemplating your footsteps — the way of the passion and of Calvary.'

5

Total Belonging to Christ

'Lord, in these days we seek to reorder the memories of our years of ministry, to consider what significance they had and, if possible, to capture the sense of our journey. Grant us the grace to carry out this action with you without running away, without bitterness, letting ourselves be assisted by the reflections made by St Paul after the years of his mission at Ephesus. May we rediscover the joy and enthusiasm of the first years, and understand the heart of pastoral living which is a sharing in your heart — the heart of the good shepherd.'

The brief underlining of the actions related in the first part of the discourse of Miletus (vv 18-21), is interesting. Paul had evidently carried out many activities in the three years passed at Ephesus yet he merely evokes those which seem relevant for himself and others: I served the Lord, I preached, instructed, witnessed. These actions are completed by attitudes — serving with humility and preaching without shrinking — on which we will reflect later.

Here we simply want to examine the actions by which Paul synthesises his whole ministry in Asia.

I served the Lord
With these words the fundamental characteristic which

marked every action is underlined; it is striking that this service is not expressed in the form of ministry-service. In fact, the Greek verb is not *diakoneō*, but *douleuō*, which means 'to serve the Lord as slave'.

1. It can be useful therefore to remember the terms Paul used to define himself in relation to his mission:

— 'But I do not account my life of any value nor as precious to myself, if only I may accomplish my course and the ministry I received from the Lord Jesus' *(Acts 20:24).*

— '...as servants of God we commend ourselves in every way' *(2 Corinthians 6:4).*

The Greek text has *diakonia* in the first case and *diakonoi* in the second.

Therefore Paul has a good understanding of this expression, as well as the other which he often uses to define himself: apostle, one sent. 'Deacon' indicates the ministerial nature of the service, 'apostle' indicates its origin:

The principal letters (1 and 2 Corinthians, Ephesians, Colossians, 1 and 2 Timothy) begin with the phrase, 'Paul, an apostle [or one sent] of Jesus Christ....'

However, there are moments — and ours is one of them — in which he defines himself as *doulos,* slave, a term not easily interchanged with 'deacon'.

We find it, for example, at the beginning of the Letter to the Romans, charged with affection and filled with hopes for the community to whom he writes: 'Paul, a slave of Jesus Christ ...'.

The Letter to the Philippians, also rich in expressions of affection and cordiality, begins with these words: 'Paul and Timothy, slaves of Jesus Christ ...'.

The Letter to the Galatians, one of the most tumultuous

regarding feelings, states: 'Am I now seeking the favour of men, or of God? If I were still pleasing men, I should not be a slave of Christ' *(1:10).*

There are, therefore, certain particularly strong moments in which the apostle does not use the ministerial definition 'deacon' nor the functional one 'apostle' but prefers a more existential definition. When he has to understand himself interiorly he uses the expression 'slave'.

2. What does the word 'slave' indicate? Certainly it denotes the awareness of total dependence on another. As Father Dupont explains so well, it is definitely not a note of servility, nor of humiliation, but it emphasises a relationship of totality: I belong wholly to the Lord. I am not simply his apostle nor his minister because my being belongs entirely to him. This is the profound root which Paul allows to surface as a memory of his ministry.

Since we wish to pass from *lectio* to *meditatio* and then to contemplative prayer, let us ask him: 'Grant that we may understand what you mean by, ''I have served the Lord'' and what you were saying when you insisted on the lordship of him who totally possessed you.'

Paul will send us to contemplate the Johannine passage of the good shepherd (John 10) which today's liturgy of St Charles offers us. Jesus, the good shepherd, proposes three fundamental human attributes relative to God.

God is favourable to me in spite of everything. That 'in spite of everything' includes sin, weakness, frailty and my incapacity. God is on my side, he is my shepherd, he worries about me, he takes care of my life, he continuously creates in me the sense of life, and instils significance into my inadequacies, confusions and my occasional bad actions. God's being favourable to us in his Son is not a secondary question for Jesus, but a question of life or death. The good shepherd risks his life and gives it for his sheep. God's being favourable to us is not an act of partial acceptance; it is a choice of totality.

God's being favourable to us is an unchanging attitude in the past, today, and forever. That is why Paul's answer becomes comprehensible to us: 'I am your slave, O Lord.' At Damascus, he had already sensed the startling reality that while he was still a sinner, a blasphemer, God was favourable to him, he was on his side until death. This is the reality that brings to birth in the heart of the Christian the desire to belong totally and radically to Jesus. Here we have the ransoming of that vague subjectivity which is ours, a subjectivity that risks growing like a cancer because it is turned in on ourselves in a dialogue with our own feelings. When I recognise the other in Christ the Lord, I am redeemed in the whole of my existence; it makes me feel saved, defined, put back into order.

'I served the Lord', is therefore an extremely rich expression. Paul served him publicly ('You know') and in a continuous and permanent manner because he lives his relationship with God, not by his own merit but by grace: 'Christ Jesus has made me his own' *(Philippians 3:12)*. He discovered that he had been sought out, loved and always welcomed and he gives himself totally.

To preach, teach and bear witness
After placing service to the Lord at the basis of Paul's pastoral experience, as we have explained it, we can easily put the other acts of ministry in their place: preaching, teaching in public and in private, bearing witness. Their aim is conversion to God and faith in Jesus Christ, but they flow forth from the experience of the apostle, they are the

evidence of his consciousness of belonging to the One who loved him even to death.

The verb *anangeilai* indicates the kerygmatic type of preaching, that is, the proclamation of the wonderful things God has accomplished for humanity in Christ. This preaching is the root of every Christian journey, the foundation of faith, the Word from which faith is born as a response in our hearts, developing into a supernatural organism and into Church.

The verb *didaxei* is catechesis, the explanation of all the consequences that the first announcement has for our behaviour, our moral actions, our living in the Church and in the world.

I leave to you the work of plumbing the depths of the verb *diamarturasthai,* seeking parallels, or, reading J. Dupont's *Exhorting Jews and Greeks* where the word 'exhort' does not give a precise indication of the contents; a better title would be *To give witness to Jews and Greeks.* Jews and Greeks signify two quite different, indeed opposite cultures, and this brings us to the problem of pluralism.

We immediately ask: How can we possibly preach to different people with the same words? It is necessary first of all to study the intrinsic nature of every culture! Here the problem is overcome by the universal character of the message that Paul reveals in his person. He makes himself a living witness before Jews and Greeks — before two hostile worlds, to believers and unbelievers, to the East and to the West, we would say — of the proclamation whose aim is conversion to God and faith in Jesus Christ, thus the acceptance of the God who is favourable to humanity, in a commitment to the crucified Lord present in the Eucharist and in the Church.

One last observation. You will have noted that in the

actions remembered by Paul we have not yet seen what we defined as typical of the discourse of Miletus: the parenesis, consolation. Perhaps it is understood in the 'exhorting' (giving witness) because it goes back to verse 31 in the section on commitment: 'Therefore, be alert, remembering that for three years I did not cease day or night to admonish everyone with tears.'

Here consolation is expressed with a new verb, in Greek *nouthetein,* but the parenetic action also serves to correct and admonish. In fact, we find the same term in Ephesians 6:4, where Paul exhorts parents: 'Fathers, do not provoke your children to angers, but bring them up in the discipline [*nouthesia*] and instruction of the Lord.' And again in 1 Corinthians 4:14, 'I do not write this to make you ashamed but to admonish you as my beloved children.' Here it is an admonishment, a correction filled with love and affection.

Points for personal prayer
We are now invited to come face to face with Paul's words, expressing our reflections in prayer.

1. Lord, in what way can I unify my ministry?

Do I really recognise the characteristics of the apostle as fundamental to what I am?

What joys, sufferings or efforts have the announcement, the *didache,* the *didaskalia,* the catechesis and the explanation given me? What joys, efforts or role do consoling and comforting give me?

The priest lives in the midst of these tasks; and he grows in charity, and therefore grows in the spiritual life, through them, when they are rooted in the choice of Christ as the one Lord, in the decision to belong totally to him alone, in making adherence to him a matter of life or death.

57

Have I served the Lord with the joyous consciousness of belonging totally to him?

Is it not true perhaps that so much of the weariness, heavinesses and frustrations which mark my day might come from not making a final decision for Christ?

2. What do we mean today by announcing, explaining, witnessing? This is certainly a real problem of the historical living out of the Christian experience. I experience joy each time my pastoral actions have the strong resonance that they had in Paul, the desire to communicate to others my basic experience. When, on the other hand, we do not manage to tune in to the proper wavelength our journey becomes uncertain, wandering. Then we become overwhelmed with problems that we may call pastoral but that are often fictitious because they are not linked to a sense of belonging to the Lord. Theology, too, in order to be authentic, must be born from Christian conversion, fired by our being caught up by the love of God in Christ.

Naturally the Lord often uses our frustration and our weariness to make us understand that we are travelling in the wrong direction. In this case, by means of repentance and prayer we can begin again, trusting ourselves to him once more.

3. In the pastoral action of comfort and consolation, do we know how to administer correctly the love that God administers to us — one of the characteristics of Paul's ministry?

Let us ask Our Lady for the gift of comparing ourselves humbly and joyously with the exemplar image of the apostle, ready to change anything within us that is still far from his example in order to be, like him, abandoned to the infinite love of God in Christ Jesus our Lord.

6

The Pastoral Service of Christ

Homily on the Solemnity of St Charles Borromeo

Today's liturgy presents the figure of St Charles above all as shepherd.

The prayer at the beginning of the liturgical assembly evokes the example and the patronage of the saint who is the 'shining gem of shepherds'. The first reading, taken from the book of the prophet Ezekiel, leads us to contemplate the theme of shepherd; the responsorial psalm is that of shepherd; the gospel acclamation takes up the words of Christ: 'I am the good shepherd'; the prayer over the gifts defines St Charles as a 'vigilant shepherd'; the preface praises God who has given to the Church an 'industrious shepherd'.

Celebrating the feast of our patron today, we do not intend simply to commemorate a few episodes of his life but rather to become aware that St Charles intercedes, with all the richness of his pastoral affection, for each one of us and for this portion of the Church for which he lived and died.

The icon of the good shepherd
Let us take up once again John 10:11-18, which begins with

the definition which Jesus gave of himself: 'I am the Good Shepherd.'

Other affirmations of the Lord come to mind: 'I am the bread of life ...' *(John 6:35)*; 'I am the light of the world ...' *(John 8:12)*; 'I am the truth ...' *(John 14:6).* These are all symbolic images which refer to concrete or abstract realities.

In our passage, however, Jesus sends us back to a person and we must therefore consider it attentively along with all the connotations of the word 'shepherd'.

In scripture, the shepherd is one who takes care of others, who solicitously guides others not only as groups but also as individuals. Therefore we are called back to the theme of educating. To educate is certainly a pastoral metaphor because it means 'to lead' the sheep from the enclosure towards the fields. Thus, for example, the Latin translation of Psalm 23 says: 'Ad aquas reflectionis educavit me.' *(Psalm 23:2)*

None the less, the figure of the shepherd in the Old Testament has a wider symbolic meaning which can also be applied to the king: the king is shepherd of the people, the one who pastures Israel. It is the image of the leader, the one who presides.

The prophet Ezekiel speaks of God as a shepherd who assumes the functions of education as well as those of leadership, who cures and consoles, who collects the dispersed and brings back the exiles. The shepherd is the provident God who guides human history, who is attentive to our fate in order to lead us out of the dark valley and bring us to the pastures of life.

The shepherd is the provident God who counts the sheep one by one; thus, each feels itself not only part of a wide universal design but the direct object of solicitous and loving attention.

This page of John's Gospel adds to the figure of the shepherd an unexpected characteristic: the offering of one's own life — a gesture of unconditional dedication. It is the extent of love for one's friends and enemies, the extent of divine charity which is honestly on our side for life and for death.

Moreover, in John 10, Jesus reveals that his loving knowledge of the sheep recalls the knowledge by which the Father knows him and he knows the Father. 'I am the good shepherd; I know my own and my own know me, as the Father knows me and I know the Father' *(John 10:14-15)*. Thanks to the provident love of God we are inserted into that same life of Trinitarian love.

The certainty of the shepherds

1. What must we draw out of our contemplation on the figure of the shepherd as it is expressed in the pages of the gospel?

Not necessarily and immediately a catalogue of duties, which would be an excessive and unbearable burden which eventually we would not be able to bear.

Even if we place such a catalogue on the shoulders of Charles and then transfer them to ourselves we would carry out an operation that in the light of Matthew 23 could be called pharisaic; we would burden ourselves with weights that are not truly our own.

In fact, today we are called to discover the providential meaning that the Lord wants to bring forth from our life history. God is my shepherd and my life is in his hands. This is the primordial act of faith that encompasses all the ulterior statements of faith. Popular wisdom called this fundamental intuition Providence. God is always with me, and on the cross today, and he gives his life for me now.

'I believe, Lord, that in all that happens to me you are on my side, that nothing can draw me away from you and that every event, good or bad, has meaning thanks to your death for me.'

St Charles lived with this certainty, abandoning himself with confidence to God who is gracious to humankind.

2. If the Lord is my shepherd then we are merely shepherds relative to Christ, in *persona Christi*. Because we depend on Jesus, all does not rest on our shoulders; the pastoral activity of the Church is representative of the action of Christ. We must be at harmony, attentive to that action which he exercises in all hearts by means of his Holy Spirit who fills every part of the earth.

Jesus has responsibility for the people; Jesus carries the weight of our ministry: the first agony was his in Gethsemane, and our every cry is but a sharing in Jesus' crying over Jerusalem or his weeping for Lazarus.

In the light of this collaboration with our humility and our weakness we participate in the pastoral service of Jesus who gives life. Let us ask St Charles to obtain for us the grace to imitate him not so much in his vigils and fasts but, above all, in his abandonment to Christ, the shepherd of his people. Let us ask for the gift of imitating him in the contemplation of the Crucified from whom he derived the certainty of being led to green pastures, in spite of all the trials that beset his life. Let us ask him for the gift of becoming worthy of participating in the ministry of Christ, of his life, his death and his cross, and in the ministry which the Holy Spirit exercises to the full in every heart.

7

Our Apostolic Awareness

'We thank you, Lord, for your gift of recalling the past, reconsidering our human and pastoral experiences from the day that we were ordained up to the present.

'We ask you to come to our aid once more that we may understand our present awareness, the knowledge that we now have of ourselves and of what lies before us.

'We know that for a believing exercise of remembering the joys and bitternesses, the graces received and our faults, the successes and failures, the ministry of reconciliation is above all useful, as it is also for a serene flowering of the knowledge of today. Grant us, Lord, to go with confidence to the sacrament of Reconciliation, to draw from it that joy and that comfort which we can then put at the disposal of our brothers and sisters.'

We have looked at various aspects of the first part of the discourse of Miletus, in particular the circumstances and the actions. We now want to go on to the second part (Acts 20:22-27) which we have called 'the awareness of the present' even though we will return later to the first part to reflect together on the attitudes proper to Paul's pastoral mission.

In fact, our subdivision of the passages is not rigorous because Paul did not speak in a precise order but allowed himself to be carried by his heart and by his feelings.

And now I go to Jerusalem

Let us begin by rereading the first verses of the second part: 'And now, behold, I am going to Jerusalem, bound in the Spirit, not knowing what shall befall me there, except that the Holy Spirit testifies to me in every city that imprisonment and afflictions await me' *(Acts 20:22-23)*.

'And now behold' indicates precisely the awareness of what Paul is living *'hic et nunc'*. When remembering the past he used the expression 'You yourselves know how I lived among you all the time from the first day...' *(Acts 20:18)*.

Awareness of the present is made up above all of certain things: 'I am going to Jerusalem, bound in the Spirit....'

'Bound in the Spirit' is a strong affirmation, which helps us to understand the depths of the apostle's emotions. The Greek text states more literally, 'tied in the Spirit', tied like a prisoner. Therefore he is going to Jerusalem without knowing the reason for his journey which none the less makes him uneasy. It frightens him but he knows without a doubt that he must go.

This is the consciousness of the great, free vocations which determine life; the consciousness of those who, having made a discernment, follow it in spite of signs of turbulence and opposition. It is not the awareness of those who simply follow orders.

Our own experience, and that of the others, can testify that the fundamental choices of life are born exactly in this way: not from a caprice, not from an emotion, but rather from an interior inspiration which makes us certain that the Lord is calling us.

They are choices which later recede, for example, in the obedience of a religious consecration, in hiddenness, in carrying out our everyday duties but which, in the beginning, were marked by this awareness.

Perhaps the modern example closest to what Paul is expressing here is that of Maximilian Kolbe who offered himself, taking a step forward in the concentration camp, feeling more repugnance than attraction, more fear than courage, but knowing that he must propose the substitution, sensing himself called to make the offer.

For Paul, 'bound in the Spirit' is another way of indicating his total belonging to Christ, his radical dependence on him who died for us on the cross, his being the 'slave' of the Lord Jesus. He could have found many excuses for not going to Jerusalem but he is attracted by the power of the Spirit which is born in the wounded heart of Christ.

Such a deep vocational feeling is clearly a grace because by ourselves we can never be faithful to our promises. It is necessary that we be conquered, be bound by the love of God in order to stay close to him. Ordinarily we cannot bind ourselves because the knots would slip too easily. Another must tie us up; Paul is bound by the Lord Jesus.

We too must grasp this liberty in our own experience. No one forced us to make this choice. We understood it as an intrinsic part of our person; we are made to give ourselves freely. This donation was not superficial, because it bound us and it binds us, it defines us and if we were to abandon it now we would be, first of all, unfaithful to ourselves, trampling on the genuine historical expression of our being.

'I am going to Jerusalem.' The dedication which

embraces the whole life of Paul is concretised in his going to Jerusalem. It is in fact a risky voyage and he takes this risk for Christ. It is a journey of charity in that he is going because of a duty of love, for the collection for his brothers, an exercise of service. It is a journey which permits him to honour the tradition of the Church of Peter and James (the great columns) and the memory of the earthly life of Jesus.

By going to Jerusalem, Paul can express his communion with the apostles and with the first community, demonstrating in this way that he is not an itinerant preacher, a founder of a new religion.

Finally, his is a journey which has the thrill of the immediate 'following' of Jesus. Acts describes him with a very clear allusion to the decision of the Lord to go to Jerusalem. Earlier, it says, after these facts (the founding of the Church of Ephesus and the first successes in that city) 'Paul resolved in the Spirit to pass through Macedonia and Achaia and go to Jerusalem' *(Acts 19:21)*.

It reminds us of the words of Luke 9:51, 'When the days drew near for him to be received up, he set his face to go to Jerusalem.'

Paul feels in some mysterious way that by going to Jerusalem, accepting the risk, seeking a link with the historical Jesus, he is obeying an interior impulse. It is the same impulse which even today brings Christians to the city of the saints to pray, to adore and to contemplate.

'Not knowing what shall befall me there', more literally, in the Greek text: 'What will happen to me I don't really know.' Here Paul's awareness refers to an uncertain and dangerous reality. The uncertainty relates most of all to the particular circumstances of his journey. Will I be accepted? How will they take my witness of charity? Will they think I want to colonise Jerusalem on behalf of the Greeks? How will the Jews treat me? Will my enemies be there?

There is uncertainty also about the results of the journey. Will my mission be fruitful? What will they think of the collection?

We must remember that Paul faced this journey at an age which, in those days, rendered him worthy of regard, of tranquillity, of a definitive settlement. The fact that he, the great model for us priests and bishops, acts in this way shakes us deeply. Above all it shakes up a culture, a way of thinking which has great need of security and support. How many times do I still hear today from religious or consecrated persons: 'What is my role? What is the task of the religious in the Church, in the parish?' Then I immediately think of the holy foundress or founder who, from heaven, is surprised to know that one of her or his children is still looking for a proper role!

The modern mentality has filled us with a fear of new tasks, particularly tasks which are not clearly defined; we are afraid to walk paths which are not clearly traced out.

All this is legitimate and we cannot joke about it, rather we should be aware that it is a part of that social frailty which we tried to discover, the fruit of a society which is deteriorating towards functionalism. Functional areas — economic, civil, military, familial and personal — are increasing, and this in turn necessitates further subdivisions of tasks, with little unity among them, each with its own internal rules. The important thing is to learn about them in order to defend our personal rights and privileges. Without being aware of it, our society is becoming ever more complicated: beneath the main ethical principles come the rules of the game which create in everyone an anxiety about meticulous definition of roles, anxiety about the future.

Naturally, we too are caught up in this mentality and we forget that the vocation of totality is not easily subdivided into precise tasks which risk suffocating the person and his or her service of the Lord Jesus; they also risk extinguishing the Spirit with clear reasoning. After all, I do have to know my role, what is expected of me!

These are the legitimations of those invited to the great banquet, and stigmatised by Jesus in the parable. It is not easy to make people understand that reasons are not absolute imperatives to which I must submit myself, that my functional relationships should be entrusted to inventiveness, to creativity, to courage, rather than to exact definitions.

Living in a society such as ours, we can admire Paul who, already old, leaves without knowing what will happen to him, and with the sole certainty that he is the servant of the Lord, one who seeks to serve him according to what the Spirit suggests.

The apostle is not interested in knowing his role, his future, the expectations of others, the rules according to which he will be given a prize or punished, promoted or rendered destitute. We find Paul fascinating because he reminds us of Abraham, the father of all believers. Faith, in fact, demands that we go beyond our plans, beyond the securities of preconceived roles, and that we begin to go forward. 'By faith Abraham obeyed when he was called to go out to a place which he was to receive as an inheritance; and he went out, not knowing where he was to go' *(Hebrews 11:8)*.

The strength of obedience, not role, defines the person. Abraham started off 'not knowing where he was going':

his was not only a theological adventure but an ethical adventure of faith. He knew who was calling him, he knew that he was called towards a country, but he did not know how and where the journey would be carried out. Evidently, without a profound awareness of call, the personality cannot survive the uncertainties of a merely pragmatic definition of self.

'Grant to us, Lord, to penetrate these words which make up our being. Let us not be concerned to defend our interests or privileges, either personal or group ones. Give us the faith and love of Abraham and of Paul.'

I also want to emphasise the dangers of a group collectivism, the mentality which degrades the spirit of the body. This too has legitimate reasons for existing because it corresponds to daily needs but when it becomes definitive and closes horizons it is the cause of much evil: the group no longer thinks of anything except defending itself, of creating space for itself; it no longer knows how to dare, to risk, to invest outside of itself.

I only know

I will limit myself to reminding you of what Paul knows of his future: 'the Holy Spirit testifies to me in every city that imprisonment and affliction await me' *(Acts 20:23).*

Besides uncertainty, the apostle foresees trials because it is difficult to follow the Crucified One without sharing his passion in some way. My episcopal motto attempts to express this awareness: *Pro veritate adversa diligere.* It is necessary to prepare oneself to love the obstacles which we will inevitably meet in the service of truth.

Paul senses it within himself and the Holy Spirit attests to it. The language is generic: imprisonment and tribulation. Imprisonment is material suffering, loss of liberty, torture, death. Tribulation is a term which refers to spiritual trials, anguish, solitude, fear, moral and psychological pressures. The word is often used in the Bible and the apostle himself recalls it in 2 Corinthians:

> Blessed be the God and Father of our Lord Jesus Christ, the Father of mercies and God of all comfort, who comforts us in all our affliction, so that we may be able to comfort those who are in any affliction... For as we share abundantly in Christ's sufferings, so through Christ we share abundantly in comfort too.' *(1:3-5)*

And further on,

> For we do not want you to be ignorant, brethren, of the affliction we experienced in Asia; for we were so utterly, unbearably crushed that we despaired of life itself. *(1:8)*

Past experiences have convinced Paul that he will suffer tribulations, and the Holy Spirit confirms it by means of prophecies, by means of the charismatic prayer of various communities. In Acts 21:11 we read of one of these premonitions, given by the prophet Agabus with a symbolic gesture:

> And coming to us he took Paul's girdle and bound his own feet and hands, and said, 'thus says the Holy Spirit, ''so shall the Jews at Jerusalem bind the man who owns this girdle and deliver him into the hands of the Gentiles.'' '

They are words pronounced after the discourse to the elders of Ephesus but Paul was thinking of this type of prophecy which he had heard.

It is interesting to note, incidentally, that the predictions could also have been accompanied by exhortations not to go to Jerusalem, thus creating a conflict of discernment between what Paul felt and what was told him by his friends, his companions in faith. In fact, it is possible — as the history of the Church shows — to receive conflicting authoritative spiritual proposals.

I do not give importance to my life

Let us begin now to reflect on the first words of Acts 20:24, where Paul returns to his affirmation of his apostolic consciousness: 'I do not account my life of any value....' This is an explanation of what he has already said: 'Serving the Lord as slave' and 'bound in the Spirit'.

No one can seriously proclaim that he attaches no importance to his own life, and we are thus faced with an understatement. This phrase makes us realise that Paul has attached a higher ideal to his life so as to be ready to risk all.

I remember some time back a person told me that he had an incurable illness yet, with great serenity, concluded 'I sleep at night all the same.' I don't mean that his condition did not matter to him but his faith in God overcame all possible distress.

Paul, with a touch of irony, is thus stating the extreme seriousness of his dedication, of his spending his life in fidelity to the ministry which, as we shall see, is 'the ministry which I received from the Lord Jesus', 'the course to be accomplished'.

Conclusion

Our personal meditation could start with a reflection carried out in a type of dialogue with the apostle. We are in fact seeking to find a continuity between our experience and

71

his, to grasp through grace the identity of the call which is his and ours, to see ourselves mirrored in him. Paul himself can be mirrored in us: we can be moved by emotion as we recognise that we are urged by the same motivations which he had at the time of the primitive Church. It is a matter of identifying ourselves in tradition, which helps us to find continuity and to express it; to rejoice in our service of dedication to Christ and of our faithful proclamation of his Gospel; to measure our apostolic awareness along Pauline lines, notwithstanding the centuries which separate us from his epoch; to quench our thirst at the fount of Jesus who gushes forth in our midst, at his Easter which touches us and reaches us.

As the Easter of Christ touched the life of Paul and called forth in him a desire, an ardour and passion for ministry, so it touches our lives today, stirring up ardour, desire and service, and liberating us from our frailty and from our sin.

Lord Jesus, let our hearts be filled with you! Do not let us say these words in vain, but let us be won by you, be bound by you. Tear from our hearts all fear, the need to have a role which, however necessary in ordinary life, can persecute us if it becomes obsessive. Grant us the liberty to serve you with humility, knowing that in every little service we symbolically reach Jerusalem — the place of your cross and resurrection — and the Church which is spread throughout the world.

8

The Counsel of God in the Life of the Priest

'Grant to us, Lord, a heart ever ready to listen. May our meditation on the words of Scripture resound as a single canticle of your crucified love for us, a canticle of you who risked your life for us and gave yourself up to death, because in every moment you faithfully love us. You, Jesus Christ, our Lord and our God who live and reign with the Father and the Holy Spirit for ever and ever. Amen.'

We have meditated on the first part of verse 24 of the discourse of Miletus; now we will read it in its entirety, remembering that we are reflecting on Paul's awareness of his present and of what awaited him:

'But I do not account my life of any value nor as precious to myself, if only I may accomplish my course and the ministry which I received from the Lord Jesus, to testify to the gospel of the grace of God.'

Let us examine these words in the light of the following ones, which convey to the presbyters the apostle's knowledge:

'And now, behold, I know...', continues the introductory interjection of this second part of the passage: '...that all you among whom I have gone about preaching the kingdom will see my face no more. Therefore I testify to you this day that I am innocent of the blood of all of you, for I did not shrink from declaring to you the whole counsel of God' *(Acts 20:25-27)*.

The particular ministries *(diakonie)*

Let us look first of all at the significance of *diakonia* — service. Here, in fact, Paul describes his ministry as 'the ministry which I received from the Lord Jesus' *(20:24)*. While in verse 19 he preferred to define it existentially, to emphasise the primacy of his total belonging to Christ, using the term slave (in Greek *douleia*) at this point he considers it necessary to deal with the question of service/*diakonia*, of particular roles.

The Synod of Bishops wanted to reflect on ministries and in a final proposition some initial suggestions about terminology were advanced, leaving the Holy See the task of going over the document *Ministeria quaedam* which instituted the ministries of lector and acolyte, to rethink it and, possibly, to rework the text.

For this reason it seems useful to pause briefly on this theme in the light of biblical teachings. In the New Testament, as we know, the word *diakonia* comes back numerous times to designate different offices: the material services rendered our neighbour, especially the serving of meals. In 2 Corinthians 8:4, the *diakonia* is the collection for the needy. The ministry of preaching is *diakonia*, by which we serve Christ above all by giving witness to him.

We can say that the New Testament uses the term *diakonia* to indicate all the offices relating to the very basic values of life (food, shelter, clothing, health, home); these services are offered for love of Christ. In the Christian, these

74

diakoniai are born of faith, they reflect the dynamism of a faith that is expressed in charity and can thus be called *diakonia ex fide*.

All the same, in particular places, at times distinct from these meanings but never separated from them, we find in the New Testament the *diakonia fidei* which has as its objective the communication of the faith: the preaching and the pastoral ministry in general by which we serve the Lord Jesus and those who hear us, offering them words of salvation.

This is the *diakonia* in the spiritual or eschatological sense that attains to ultimate values.

The diakonia of Paul

The exegetes naturally asked what *diakonia* Paul was alluding to when he said: 'If only I may accomplish my course and the ministry which I received from the Lord Jesus'.

1. If we begin with the context, we must reply that it is a temporal service: the apostle is bringing to Jerusalem the collection to which he has been deeply committed, even on his honour, from the communities of Macedonia and Achaia. He wants a happy outcome of the collection affair: he has the money and wants to bring it to Jerusalem himself. Naturally he is moved by charity, by the needs of the poor of Jerusalem. The faithful of Macedonia and Achaia were not rich but they willingly collected, on Sunday — the first day of the week — something to send to those who had less than they, in imitation of Christ who made himself poor for us so that we could be rich with his richness (2 Corinthians 8:9).

Besides being a *diakonia* of charity it is also a *diakonia* of communion, which Oscar Cullman would call 'ecumenical'. Paul intends demonstrating that among the communities of Greece, which seem to be developing without taking tradition into account, there is no discordance with regard to the older communities of Jerusalem which were tied more closely to the sphere of the law. Paul is worried and tries to avoid a split which seems to be emerging between the so-called 'Judaeo-Christian' and the Hellenic-Christian communities.

Time would, unfortunately, prove him right. The Church would soon be without the lymph of the Judaeo-Christian community that was, in itself, growing in such a promising way. For this reason there are those today who see in the reflowering of the Judaeo-Christian community in Jerusalem a providential sign for a return to the conditions of the primitive Church made up of Greek and Jew. We must take to heart the problem of the chosen people, not only because Jesus was born from them but, above all, because at the beginning of Christianity they formed a preponderant, integral part of the Christian community.

2. The context of the discourse of Miletus indicates, none the less, that the first meaning of Paul's service is the specific apostolic *diakonia* spoken of, for example, in Acts where Judas is remembered: 'For he was numbered among us and was allotted his share in this ministry [*diakonia*]' *(Acts 1:17)*. And, immediately afterwards, when the apostles pray to the Lord for the choice of a disciple who will take the place of the Iscariot: 'Lord who knowest all hearts, show which one of these two thou has chosen to take the place in this ministry [*diakonia*] and apostleship' *(Acts 1:24)*.

The majority of exegetes maintain that Paul, speaking

to the elders of Ephesus, is alluding above all to this apostolic *diakonia* which is very important to him and which he had defended strongly in 2 Corinthians (in 1 Corinthians and in the Letter to the Romans, he also insisted that he possessed the apostolic *diakonia*).

In reality, the context of Acts does not seem to apply to the collection, which is mentioned for the first time in chapter 20 and which does not have to do with Ephesus but, as we said, with the communities of Macedonia and Achaia. The presbyters of Ephesus as presented to us seem to be ignorant of this matter.

Besides, the way in which Paul defines diakonia here clearly indicates that we are speaking of that service 'which I received from the Lord Jesus to testify to the gospel of the grace of God'. It is true that at a certain point it implies the management of the *diakonia* of the collection; but it is above all a witness to the message of grace, thus the proclamation of the gospel of mercy on which we will reflect later.

3. This diakonia was confided to Paul by the Lord Jesus and is part of his human, historical authenticity. When was it confided to him? He was probably thinking of his conversion-vocation to which he always referred when he spoke of the origin of his mission.

'He who had set me apart before I was born...' *(Galatians 1:15)*.

Having received this *diakonia* from the Lord Jesus, he never loses courage:

'Therefore, having this ministry by the mercy of God, we do not lose heart' *(2 Corinthians 4:1)*. 'Such is the confidence that we have through Christ toward God. Not that we are sufficient of ourselves to claim anything as

77

coming from us; our sufficiency is from God who has qualified us to be the ministers [*diakonoi*] of a new covenant, not in a written code but in the Spirit *(2 Corinthians 3:4-6).'*

In conclusion, Paul expresses the awareness of his own *diakonia* in various ways; serving the Lord as slave, preaching, announcing the will of God, admonishing, proclaiming the kingdom.

I know that you will see my face no more

I offer some further thoughts for your work of meditation on the second part of the passage — that of Paul's knowledge of the present.

Verse 25 begins: 'And now behold, I know that you will see my face no more', words which make this discourse a testament.

In so far as we can deduce from his life and his pastoral letters, the apostle then returned to Miletus. However, as happens at the important moments of life, he looks to the future and wants to express his thoughts with clarity, communicating all that he has in his heart, without reticence, as if it were for the last time.

'Therefore I testify to you this day that I am innocent of the blood of all of you' *(v 26).* Coming face to face with this affirmation can surprise us. This is not a moralistic self-vindication; it is rather a complex evaluation of one who, in spite of everything, feels that he has given himself completely, that he has given his all for others. It is therefore a profound demonstration of affection towards the community and towards the individuals who form it.

It reminds me of the beautiful writing of Paul VI in *Thoughts of Death* where, overcoming the modesty that usually restrained him, the pontiff exclaims: 'I could say that I have always loved the Church... and it seems to me that I have lived for her, not for anything else. But I would like the Church to know this, and I would like to have the strength to share what is in my heart in a way that one can only have the courage to do at the very end of one's life.' It is the sure awareness of one who has given his life.

Perhaps in prayer we can sense what the apostle intended when he said that he gave all. Perhaps it will be given us to enter into his heart to understand with what tenderness and participation he lived his ministry.

At a certain point he becomes almost proud of what he had done, but it is the pride of a father who says: 'I have indeed done everything for you.' His having done all is expressed in a strong metaphor: 'I am innocent of the blood of all of you'. Paul foresees, first of all, that some will probably be lost and therefore admonishes the presbyters: 'Will you all keep faith with this word?'

The admonishment is strengthened by verse 29: 'After my departure fierce wolves will come in among you, not sparing the flock.' The wolves will seem like shepherds; it is easy for us to understand the drama of what is being said as well as the strength of his awareness that he is not to blame if someone is lost.

We, rightly, prefer to blame ourselves always, especially for those confided to our pastoral care, who at a certain point go away: children, young people, people who die without the sacraments, adults who leave the faith.

Paul has the knowledge of the shepherd who, coming to the end, feels that he has succeeded by the grace of God in accomplishing all.

He accomplished everything because he announced the will of God. The expression returns twice: 'I have gone about preaching the kingdom' (v 25), and 'I did not shrink from declaring to you the whole counsel of God' *(v 27)*.

The formula of verse 25 does not occur elsewhere in Paul. At times he speaks of the kingdom of God but he never designates his preaching as 'the preaching of the kingdom' which, instead, is typical of the gospels. The centre of the apostle's preaching is Jesus, the Lord, Kyrios, Jesus risen, and conversion to him.

Luke probably intended to make a connection with Acts 19:8, 'And he entered the synagogue' of Ephesus, where he, Paul 'for three months spoke boldly, arguing and pleading about the kingdom of God', and chapter 28: 'And he lived there two whole years at his own expense, and welcomed all who came to him, preaching the kingdom of God and teaching about the Lord Jesus Christ' *(Acts 28:30-31)*.

Luke wanted to underline the continuity between the preaching of the Teacher and that of his disciples. The expression 'kingdom of God' is not a verbal equivalent to the formula 'Jesus dead and risen'; however, the author of the Acts teaches us that the new version of the Pauline message leaves the substance of the proclamation intact. Jesus announces the kingdom of God, but this kingdom begins on earth with his death and resurrection, with our adherence to the paschal mystery.

Even the term 'counsel of God' demands a certain reflection because the text reads: 'I did not shrink from declaring to you the *whole* counsel of God.'

We mentioned, in the part in which Paul recalls the past, that along with circumstances and actions he remembers attitudes, in all humility and without shrinking. This latter signals the courage needed for announcing: a courage so great that we are tempted to retreat. What strikes us most, however, is that it speaks of the whole counsel of God, of the whole divine plan; the expression is certainly excessive because this design, in part, has not yet been revealed. Father J. Dupont observes that emphasis should be placed on the words 'to you' and 'announce to you'.

It makes us think that the announcement of the *whole* counsel of God to the presbyters is one which refers particularly to them, which touches them and is part of their ministry. Dupont refers to two texts which add some clarity:

Firstly, Luke 7:29-30, where Jesus comments on the preaching of John the Baptist: 'When they heard this, all the people and the tax collectors justified God, having been baptised with the baptism of John; but the Pharisees and the lawyers rejected the purpose of God for themselves, not having been baptised by him.'

This does not refer to the general plan of God but rather to that plan, by which, through baptism and a public confession of sin, he was to reach the Pharisees and the doctors of the law in their ethical existence, in their personal life. It is a counsel of God about human behaviour, not simply the revelation of important divine decisions.

The second text is in Acts 13:36, 'For David, after he had served the counsel of God in his own generation, fell asleep, and was laid with his fathers, and saw corruption.' Here too the reference is not to the plan of God but to the counsel of God for David.

The task of the presbyters
We can therefore conclude that the serious task from which Paul did not shrink — his pastoral letters give many examples of this — is all the difficult moral exhortation which derives from the gospel. Among others there is the passage in Timothy 3:2-3: 'Now a bishop must be above reproach, the husband of one wife, temperate, sensible,

dignified, hospitable, an apt teacher, no drunkard, not violent but gentle, not quarrelsome and no lover of money.'

This is obviously a particular consideration for the *episcopoi* of the community, we would say for the 'presbyterial college'. It was tiresome to recommend to Timothy: 'Have nothing to do with godless and silly myths. Train yourself in godliness; for while bodily training is of some value, godliness is of value in every way' *(1 Timothy 4:7-8)*. 'Attend to the public reading of scripture, to preaching, to teaching. Do not neglect the gift you have, which was given to you by prophetic utterance when the elders laid their hands upon you. Practise these duties, devote yourself to them so that all may see your progress. Take heed to yourself and to your teaching; hold to that for by doing so you will save both yourself and your hearers' *(1 Timothy 4:13-16)*.

They are words which, said sadly and lovingly, make Paul aware of not having shrunk from his task, of not having soothed the presbyters with ideologies instead of indicating to them even the small things that constitute the counsel of God in their lives and ours.

Taken in themselves, they could have appeared to be a parenesis separated from the kerygma; but coming from the heart of Paul, slave of the Lord Jesus, preacher of Jesus and of his paschal mystery, they become the practical mark of the gospel in life and in daily discipline, in prayer, in the custody of the senses, in attention to time, in living honestly one's commitments, in taking care of one's health, one's time, in not overworking.

They are the concrete ways of living according to the gospel of divine grace which Paul — setting himself as the example and model of the presbyters and of all of us — recommends to us by his life and by his ministry.

Help us, Paul, to understand all these words of yours so that they may fall on us as a light burden that unifies us in the vision of the kingdom, in the love of Christ. Give us the certainty that our existence does not reach its fullness through easy ideologies or empty slogans but through love, through faithfulness to the Word, and to the way of life of our Lord Jesus.

9

The Gospel of Grace

Homily for the Mass of Thursday, 31st Week of the Year

Reflecting in the last meditation on Paul's apostolic *diakonia* or ministry, we said that according to the definition given in Acts 20:24, it was above all a proclamation of the gospel of mercy or grace: 'I do not account my life of any value nor as precious to myself, if only I may accomplish my course and the ministry which I received from the Lord Jesus, to testify to the gospel of the grace of God.'

This statement merits deeper study because it is beautiful and rich in significance.

Providentially, the gospel passage of the daily liturgy (Luke 15:1-10) constitutes an exemplification in parable of the 'message of the grace of God' and therefore can also help us to respond to the question: 'What does it mean today to bear witness to the gospel of grace?'

The parable of mercy

First of all, Luke's text emphasises that the gospel of grace has not been understood. In fact, the scribes and the pharisees complain because all the publicans and sinners draw near to Jesus to listen to him: 'This man receives sinners and eats with them' *(Luke 15:2)*.

The complaints come from those who live out their religious practices and who consider that they have acquired rights in relation to the kingdom of God. All the same, their opposition to the gospel of grace of Jesus is not made directly but through allusions, whisperings, vague references, little phrases containing half-truths that are spread around and misunderstood. It seems that Jesus spends all his time with sinners.

To speak a half-truth, with all that it implies, is the way in which the gospel of grace has always been opposed in the Church.

Jesus does not defend himself but simply restates the message of divine mercy because the word of God is light and does not need to be illuminated by others.

We do not have time to contemplate the parable of the lost sheep and the silver coin lost by the woman and then found. We will limit ourselves to observing that, together with the parable of the prodigal son (today's liturgy omits it) they express the truth of a call of salvation that is concerned with each of us, with every individual. For those who dream of a Christianity with some kind of cosmic programme worked out in advance, of a Christianity that cannot stop to seek out a lamb or a silver coin or a child who has left the family home, it will be difficult to accept the gospel of grace.

I would like to point out, moreover, that the parable demonstrates a type of obstinacy on the part of the shepherd, the woman and the father. The God of mercy, in fact, takes the individual to heart as if that individual were the only person in existence, saying as it were: 'You are important to me; I miss you, for you I put my life on the line.'

Finally, Jesus insists on the *joy* of the finding. It becomes the dominant theme, in juxtaposition to the tears of the search; when the lamb is found the shepherd 'lays it on his shoulders, rejoicing. And when he comes home, he calls together his friends and his neighbours saying to them "Rejoice with me, for I have found my sheep which was lost." ' The woman finding the silver coin 'calls together her friends and neighbours saying "Rejoice with me, for I have found the coin which I had lost." '

In both cases — as in that of the prodigal son — the conclusion is the same: 'Just so, I tell you, there will be more joy in heaven over one sinner who repents than over ninety-nine righteous persons who need no repentance' *(v 7)*. 'Just so, I tell you there is joy before the angels of God over one sinner who repents' *(v 10)*. This gospel of the grace of God touches each of us, because we continually risk being lost or misguided and we are continually sought with love by him who repeats, 'I am interested precisely in you, in your life'.

The demands of the gospel of grace

Putting ourselves now on the side of the complainers, we can ask ourselves: Doesn't the gospel of mercy in the end become a gospel of triviality, of permissiveness, of ethical non-involvement?

Perhaps at times we have repeated the words of the pharisees or have listened to others express fear about a message that seems to endanger the observance of the law, the rigour of tradition or the doctrinal and moral securities of a group. This is a serious matter and we must not allow these doubts to penetrate our hearts, for then we would no longer understand the gospel of grace. Here we must implore light from the Lord in prayer.

I offer, none the less, some reflections which you can deepen.

God does not change; whatever the consequences we might fear, he is the God of mercy.

Fears about this gospel of grace expresses perhaps a fear of submitting to this rule. I think of Dietrich Bonhoeffer who, for all his protestant tradition, could be said to have given in to the gospel of grace and who felt the need to call it 'grace at a high price'. There can be a hidden repugnance in us toward accepting God as he is, toward letting ourselves be invaded by his mercy. We prefer to defend ourselves with the law, with justice, with the ethical rigour of the gospel. There can be within us only a partial understanding of the gospel of grace and thus, instinctively, we estrange ourselves from it.

The gospel of grace has in the one who receives it the mark of gratuity. There is nothing more pressing than gratuity, exactly because, contrary to the gospel of the law, it has no limits — I am not obliged, I am not my brother's keeper!

The demand of the gospel of grace goes beyond all laws and all roles because it touches us in the depths of our being and invites us to give ourselves, even to death.

When the gospel of grace is not heeded, we are seized in the grip of discontent and desperation. It does not force us to give ourselves, to forget our own egoism, but it leaves us free to close ourselves into our own desperation in a total rejection and thus to lose ourselves in our own personal or group solitude, in a defence that goes to extremes, until we realise that there is nothing to defend.

Grant to us, Lord the grace of understanding the demands, the openings and the horizons of your gospel of grace. Put it into our hearts and into our lives, as it was in the heart and life of Paul.

Mary, full of grace, most perfect icon of the gospel of grace, give us a knowledge of ourselves and of our Church as witnesses in the world of grace of the gospel.

10

Be Alert

Lord Jesus, today we listen to the words which you repeat to each of us through Paul, 'Be alert'. Grant us the grace to exercise ourselves especially in alertness in these days of retreat in order not to let ourselves be surprised by feelings and fantasies, not to let ourselves be led astray by superficiality and fatigue.

Grant that we may not merit your reproach: 'Could you not watch with me one hour?' (cf. Matthew 26:40). You, Lord, keep watch in your Church, and in agony until the end of the world. Grant that we may unite ourselves to the watchfulness of those who are in prison, especially those who are there because of their faith.

Grant that we may unite ourselves with the watchfulness of those who have incurable illnesses and who perhaps struggle against being overcome by despair. Grant that we may unite ourselves with the watchfulness of those who hunger and thirst for food, for justice, for dignity. Accept our humble offering in union with your vigil in Gethsemane and with your cross for the salvation of all of this humanity which is dear to us and that you have commended to us. You, who live and reign, intercede for us with the Father for ever and ever.

We have arrived at the third part of the discourse of Miletus: the commitment, or what is properly called *parenesis* to the presbyters (vv 28-31): 'Take heed to yourselves and to all the flock, in which the Holy Spirit has made you guardians, to feed the Church of the Lord which he obtained with his own blood. I know that after my departure fierce wolves will come in among you, not sparing the flock; and from among your own selves will arise men speaking perverse things, to draw away the disciples after them. Therefore, be alert, remembering that for three years I did not cease night or day to admonish every one with tears.'

The parenesis
In reality, we have seen that the whole Pauline discourse is parenetic because the apostle, speaking of himself, invites others to reflect on their presbyterial experience and then consoles them, confirms them, exhorts them and encourages them, even by means of admonishment.

In the third part, however, the specific aspect of parenesis is explicit, as we can note from the use of the imperative 'Be alert'. In Paul's letters we can distinguish general exhortations (addressed to all the faithful) from specific exhortations (addressed to particular categories or regarding defined problems). For example, we find a general parenesis in Romans 12-15 and in Ephesians 4-6.

Here we are interested in the specific parenesis given by the apostle to the presbyters and bishops, keeping in mind that these two terms are interchangeable. From the letters most similar to the discourse of Miletus we would draw attention, for example, to 1 Timothy 3:1-13, where Paul speaks to the bishops and deacons; 2 Timothy 2:14-26 and 4:1-5; Titus 1:5-14 and 3:8-11.

We also have an example of specific parenesis to the elders, that is to the presbyters of the Church, in 1 Peter 5:1-4.

The parenesis is suggested by a specific situation and expresses that which can be useful in a certain moment. 'I did not shrink from declaring to you anything that was profitable' *(Acts 20:20)*.

At times I have had someone say to me after a homily as I am sure, has happened to you, 'I expected you to speak of the Trinity' or 'I thought you would have referred to the situation in Nicaragua', and so on. Parenesis is a precise choice and it is wrong to expect a homily to be about what we ourselves are thinking of.

Paul therefore emphasises certain things which, in his judgement, are timely for the presbyters.

Reflecting on his words, let us try to understand who the presbyters of Ephesus are and exactly what exhortations the apostle addresses to them.

The presbyters of Ephesus

In Paul's time a presbyter or elder was a person between the ages of thirty-five and forty-five. In fact, at fifty, one was already old.

The primitive Church used the term to refer to people already mature in the faith, people who had acquired a certain steadiness and who could therefore be trusted. In a patriarchal society, it is easy enough to identify the person who, step by step, has acquired a certain authoritativeness and on whom you can rely.

Paul, who finds himself at Miletus, calls for these elders, he gathers them together in a room or, more probably, in the open, in a courtyard.

1. How can we imagine them? Sitting on the ground, wrapped in their cloaks, a bit tired from a three-day journey under the heat of the sun and three nights passed uncomfortably. Most of them must have been workers,

91

persons of rough build, who had strong muscles and long beards, with different colouring — Greeks and Asiatics — because they lived in a city which was a cultural frontier. Perhaps there was a civil servant or an ex-rabbi among them.

We see them attentive and probably a bit intimidated. Paul was spoken of as one who preached well, who spoke just words, but also as one who was restless, tormented, uncomfortable.

Looking at this group of presbyters, we think immediately of a group of leaders. Sociologically they are laity, perhaps many are married and have a regular job. We can compare them to a pastoral council in a country parish.

Only a few are full-time or itinerant 'evangelists' who for some years carry out services in the community; or perhaps they study scripture while the community supports them.

Nonetheless, canonically they are priests, and are even called bishops. They take turns presiding over the Eucharist when the apostle is not present; they administer baptism; they direct catechesis and they occupy themselves with the converts. One of them takes care of administration and others look after difficult marriages. They give advice, bring peace when there are arguments among various groups in the community and they meet periodically to deal together with the principal problems that arise.

At this time the apostles are still alive and thus the community is an apostolic and not an episcopal one. When the apostle is far away they write to him about serious problems or they consult with him as they did at Miletus.

2. Our efforts to imagine them evidently does not

encompass the whole reality and it is worth summarising the data collected by exegesis.

I will base myself on the great Catholic writer, H. Schürmann, who has dedicated himself during these last years to preaching — particularly to priests — and to reflecting on spirituality. Keeping in mind his exegesis on this subject, I propose four fundamental considerations to illuminate the figure of the presbyter.

i) The first Christians live in communities that are quite small, except for the community of Jerusalem which includes several thousand people. The communities are called churches; in some cases they are called 'fraternities' (cf 1 Peter 2:17).

Fraternal love is the characteristic of those communities according to the exhortation in Romans 12:10: 'Love one another with brotherly affection'. The term 'brotherly' indicates the spirit that must reign in a large family, which is precisely what the community is.

They organise themselves to carry out fraternal services which are divided up among the members of the community. The diversity of the *diakoniai* or ministries must not violate the fundamental equality that exists in the community. Paul insists on emphasising that all of the services are ordained for the growth of everyone (cf 1 Corinthians 12:5).

ii) In this context of the primitive community, the presbyters (sometimes called bishops) are the faithful who have the diakonia of presiding. They exercise it as members of a presbyterium or body of presbyters.

Thus we are speaking of a group, cited for example in 1 Timothy 4:14 where it states: 'Do not neglect the gift you have, which was given you by prophetic utterance when the elders laid their hands upon you.'

This presbyterial college intervenes above all in certain key moments: the presidency of the Eucharist, admission of others to the college through the imposition of hands; admission to baptism, decisions on cases causing grave scandal.

Among the presbyters, there are prophets and doctors (cf Acts 13:1), those who have the gift of preaching or of teaching scripture. In this context it is interesting to read 1 Timothy 5:17: 'Let the elders who rule well be considered worthy of double honour, especially those who labour in preaching and teaching' (notice the emphasis on labouring). Despite this, a prophet or doctor is not necessarily a presbyter. A presbyter is above all a person with responsibility.

iii) The call to the presbyterial college requires certain spiritual and ascetical dispositions in the candidate. A measure of fraternal love that was above normal; a greater degree of availability for service (the ability to renounce one's own time of relaxation, of work, etc.); a good capacity for human relationships in order to be able to act as a member of a group together with the apostle for the construction and maintenance of the community fraternity. It was not full-time work, nor was a celibate condition required. The college of presbyters always acts in reference to the apostle, to the founder of the community who goes to visit them, to animate them, to exhort them.

With the disappearance of the apostles, the figure of the bishop emerges; he is chosen from among the presbyters and exercises the authority proper to the apostle.

iv) The numerical development of the Church provoked the birth of the present-day episcopal or diocesan Churches or particular Churches which included large fraternities for whose service presbyters were ordained.

The state of the presbyter has thus undergone sociological change, as has that of the bishop. Since about fifteen centuries ago they have exercised a ministry that is much more demanding, much more intense in responsibility, than the ministries of the first presbyters of Ephesus. At that time, even if in their hearts they were called to a radical following of Christ, sociologically they remained laity. The priestly state took shape in the third and fourth centuries, in the progressive evolution of the Church and the increase in the needs of worship and in organisational and cultural demands.

More and more the priest, in his dedication, came to resemble the apostles called to leave all in order to follow Christ. He resembled less and less the elders of the assembly of Ephesus. We may say that we are like Paul, Peter, Luke, Silas and Timothy, who consecrated themselves body and soul to evangelisation and to the service of the community.

The priest slowly assumed the spiritual style of those who became disciples of Jesus, that is, called to follow him, they left their nets and their families. There were evidently different nuances and degrees in their sociological insertion into the ongoing life of the Church.

This new condition did not completely exclude a trade; Paul himself maintained his work, but factors other than his trade determined his choices.

Basically the vocation that the apostle lived, as slavery to the Lord, is expressed today by priests in different forms that are, never the less, much more demanding than those asked of the primitive presbyterial college.

Watchfulness in the New Testament
Paul's parenesis to the elders of Ephesus has a key word: 'Take heed ... be alert' *(vv 28, 31).*

95

Let us look briefly at the general significance of the attitude of alertness, of its evocative power in the New Testament.

1. If we examine the Greek text, we realise that the verbs translated in the Italian version of the Bible are very different, although both give the same exhortation.

The 'take heed' of v 28 is *prosechete*. It means 'to pay attention to', 'to have to do with'. It can be used in a positive sense as, for example, in 1 Timothy 4:13: to be dedicated to reading, attend to reading; or in the negative sense as in Matthew 6:1: 'Beware of not practising your piety before men.'

The 'be alert' of v 31 is translated *gregoreite,* and it means to wake up, to be in that state of awareness of one who has already slept well. It occurs often in the New Testament. There is the alertness of fear (the owner is afraid that thieves will come and he keeps watch); there is the alertness of awe (the servant is concerned that his master returning will find him sleeping or drunk with his friends); there is the alertness of the bride who awaits her spouse — this is the idea of the Canticle of Canticles and it is also implicit in the parable of the ten virgins. She who awaits the spouse keeps her lamp burning; thus it is an alertness of desire: Come Lord Jesus! We have the alertness of the liturgy: We await your return! And, finally, it is the alertness of friendship, that to which Jesus invites his apostles.

2. All these meanings of alertness or watchfulness suggest to us its importance. We must keep watch because if we fall asleep spiritually we may be surprised by the devil, by sin, by sexual appetite, by an explosion of sensuality,

by temptation, by fantasy, by curiosity. At times we fall into serious unexpected weaknesses and it is precisely because, having prayed, we presumed that we had nothing further to worry about, forgetting the frailty that always accompanies us.

The Church tells us to be alert: in order not to be surprised by death while we are in sin; to invoke the coming of the kingdom of God in the world, the return of the Lord; to accompany Jesus in his agony by praying at length and thus purifying ourselves of vain or sinful desires.

3. This alertness in awaiting the Lord is the typical attitude of the person of the Bible, of the person of evangelical hope, of the person who does not settle into present securities but who reaches towards the future. For this reason, the New Testament evokes the theme of alertness by other verbs besides the two recalled by Paul in our passage: Mark 13:33 where 'be alert' is translated by a Greek word which means 'fighting sleepiness'.

To the exhortation to be alert is often added the invitation to unceasing prayer, prayer without end. The so-called prayer of the Russian pilgrim, or the Jesus Prayer, in which the invocation of the name of Jesus is constantly repeated with the lips, the mind and the heart, leads us to an alertness in daily life.

Even the recommendation to 'be sober' is in line with alertness because wine makes our mind heavy and sleepy.

Our alertness
Today we live in a world that does not sense the possible weight of the return of the Lord as it was felt in the time of the first Christians. Our epoch is more fearful of an atomic war and the nuclear forces which could destroy

humanity. This fear moves many people, especially the young, to fight against possible world conflicts, against arms. We are present at a secular translation of the waiting, which in the framework of the New Testament hope is a waiting for the Spouse who comes.

The fear of the end is interpreted and purified because it corresponds to an existential, permanent attitude of humanity: history will have an end, the things of this earth will be overturned.

Another fear particularly prevalent in our society is caused by thieves, by robbers: we defend ourselves with padlocked doors, we hire the services of private security guards or even bodyguards. This sense of alertness too is a secularised expression of the awaiting of the Parousia.

But what does this evangelical alertness mean for us? I offer a few starting points for your personal meditation:

1. Alertness is an awaiting for the divine who already comes in me, who is manifesting himself in me and in the world. Hence the importance of being alert to the signs of the times, to the motions of the Spirit, to personal spiritual discernment, and to pastoral discernment. In this way, we recover that New Testament alertness.

2. The heart which awaits the spouse is alert: it senses his footsteps, it notes his drawing near and jumps with joy, in tune with the signs of his coming. It is the alertness lived in the liturgy starting with the great paschal vigil and prolonged in silent prayer, in meditation, in the *lectio divina*.

3. This alertness must be learned and taught. Even though it is a profound existential attitude of the spirit, it is necessary to purify it, to enlighten it by means of the word of God. I am thinking of the time of retreat, of days

of recollection, of discipline in prayer. Retreats should become a pastoral method, a point of reference to accustom ourselves to a more attentive and continuous watchfulness in the area of fantasy, of our senses, of our affections and to a discernment which will very shortly cause our life to mature.

Grant to us, Lord, not to be sleepy or drowsy at your return. And because you come now, come at any moment, come always, help us to be alert and to keep watch over ourselves and over all that we do in our daily round.

11

Attentiveness to Christ and to the Church

'Lord, you keep watch over us always. Grant to us, Father, to be able to keep watch with your Son in the hour of passion and trials. Grant to us to keep watch in the hour of passion of the world and of the Church. Enlighten our intelligence so that we will know how to protect ourselves from darkness and evil and how to follow Jesus Christ, your Son, Our Lord in all that we do.'

Now we would like to reflect on the particular circumstances of remaining alert, which we have considered to be an attitude proper to Christian living. As we hold Paul's exhortation before us, we ask ourselves various questions in order to understand how it affects us today:

—Over whom were the presbyters of Ephesus, those responsible for the community, to keep watch?
—Why must they keep watch?
—How must they do this?

'Take heed to yourselves and all the flock'
Paul does not recommend that the elders heed only themselves or the flock. He leaves no room for certain types

of ideological overlaps such as: take care of yourselves and you will take care of your flock, or, look after the flock and you will thus look after yourselves. Here we are confronted with a dialectic that cannot be eliminated: *you/the flock*. A priest who does not pray, who does not find time to read, who does not find time for his spiritual life, cannot cite as an excuse his unceasing service to his people. In reality he is keeping watch over the flock but not over himself.

Likewise, he cannot detach himself from the needs of his flock, saying that he dedicates his day to prayer, to reading, to the study of theology. In this way he would be keeping watch over himself but not over his flock.

The two are related; they enrich each other reciprocally; they complete each other but are not confused. We are always tempted to fall into this error, to find other solutions, to eliminate one of the two poles that Paul emphasises with such simplicity.

The dialectic, I/the others, internal/external, heaven/earth, the penultimate/the ultimate, belongs to created existence and we must accept it and live it patiently, continually seeking the right balance. Only in this way will we know that in serving ourselves we serve our communities, and in serving our community we grow in faith, hope and love to a far greater extent than if we dedicated months to planning a project of spiritual life.

'Take heed to yourselves and to all the flock' (v *28*): let us take care of ourselves and, at the same time, take care of others.

The place at stake
Paul gives two motives for exhorting to vigilance.

1. One motive is the importance of the place at stake.

'Take heed to yourselves and to all the flock, in which the Holy Spirit has made you guardians, to feed the Church of the Lord which he obtained with his own blood.'

The exegetes discuss whether 'his' blood is intended as the blood of the Son; in any case, it is clear that what is in question is the passion and redeeming death of Jesus, the love of God, even unto death, for this his flock in the midst of which the Holy Spirit has placed the presbyters, the bishops.

Here Paul evokes the mystery of the Trinity in which we are involved; we can thus reflect at length in prayer on the depth of this expression.

2. A second motive is that of the incumbent dangers. 'I know that after my departure fierce wolves will come in among you, not sparing the flock; and from among your own selves will arise men speaking perverse things, to draw away the disciples after them' (vv *29-30*).

The departure to which Paul alludes is probably his death, a departure without return. The Greek word is actually more indicative of an arrival and it did not belong to contemporary usage. Some exegetes suppose that Luke employed it above all to signify the solemnity of the moment.

Fierce wolves will come in: the Greek text has a term that is not easy to explain because it means literally 'heavy wolves'. Perhaps it refers to werewolves, a monstrous and terrifying reality. In their cruelty they do not spare even the flock. Paul seems shocked that these wolves molest not only the presbyters who are more mature and more prepared but also the simple faithful who have no defences.

These wolves will enter in *among you*. The warning is so serious as to induce the apostle to strengthen it: *even* in the midst of you. There will be attacks from the outside, persons who come to harm you. But men will come forth even from the heart of your community — from your presbyterium that I formed with so many tears — to spread aberrations: 'There will arise men speaking perverse things.'

Therefore the picture is dark and desolate; however, it is not an isolated case in the New Testament. In the letters of Peter and James we find a description of these masters of error, swollen like clouds without water, carried by the wind; evil people, perverse, deceitful, seducers, capable of attracting disciples and thus causing the growth of new and evil forms of discipleship. Even in Paul's pastoral letters we are presented with an obscure and gloomy picture. We could say that while the Apostle appears optimistic and confident in his first letters, towards the end of his life he becomes tense and worried, noticing the presence of errors that ruin the field for him, that turn the vineyard upside down, that spoil the sowing. Actually, Paul is controversial right from the beginning but the tone of the last documents makes us think.

Who are these men, where do they come from and what do they say? Are they heretics? Schismatics? Are they persons who ruin doctrine or who create separate groups, dividing the Church?

The text provides us with no answer but Paul provokes us to reflection because his words were written for the Church of all times, and therefore they were also written for us.

Watch out for errors

1. These persons, symbolised by fierce wolves, seem to come from other Christian communities. Their doctrine

is not identified with pagan errors — corruption from the world, secularisation, indifference, atheist philosophies. Paul is preoccupied with errors that develop in the midst of the Church, errors brought about by persons who want to insinuate themselves into the communities formed and founded by him.

There are also, however, people born into the faith in the fraternity of Ephesus, who teach perverse doctrine causing divisions and arguments.

From the description we understand that these people can be divided into two categories:

—pseudo-teachers, learned cultured people who are able to speak with a certain dialectic penetration. They are the ones who attract attention, interest and curiosity, who know how to get others to listen to them.

—leaders, people of strong temperament capable of imitating others, people who have a certain lust for spiritual power over others, who like to dominate. This lust is more dangerous than material domination because it is more subtle and more perverse.

Paul's warning puts us on guard above all against ourselves, because each of us can become a pseudo-teacher or a pseudo-leader who, instead of helping others to grow, dominates them, puts others at our service, makes them instruments of our own pride: and each of us can become a teacher who goes astray.

Paul also helps us to understand which doctrines go astray from the true faith. The hypotheses of the exegetes are many and they make use, above all, of information taken from the letters that the apostle wrote while in prison. The letters to the Ephesians and to the Colossians furnish data on the errors of Ephesus and Asia.

Besides these, the hypotheses are based also on the letters of St John who, when he speaks of these themes, is quite free with insults and even with curses and threats. In the older Christian literature, we have also St Ignatius of Antioch and St Irenaeus.

2. For our work during the retreat, it is important to stress three points:

i) The difficulty in accepting the straightforward and sole mediation of Christ. It is one of the causes underlying the problems of those coming from the Jewish religion, good, religious people who were quite fervent. The need for visible or multiple mediation, or for imaginary mediation which fills the universe in order not to leave the believer alone before God, to defend him from direct contact with Jesus, from the strength of his personal love, is at the basis even of the errors which wind in and out of Colossus and Ephesus.

Therefore, it is not a purely intercessory mediation (as, for example, in the devotions to Our Lady and the saints) but is, rather, constitutive: the mediation of angels or powers, of aeons or ages. These are all systems of security which are quite amazing.

I believe, however, that the luxuriousness of pseudo-religion or mystical fantasy can interest even the contemporary person. In fact, the fear of a simple contact with Christ Love, who can ask everything of me always, gives rise to a need to protect myself with intermediate systems that we can control.

ii) The ascetic type of exaggeration which give the impression of great severity, of a tangible sanctity. More than once Paul denounces the error of a religiosity based on the negation of our corporeity, on the pretext of anticipating the final state of resurrection, living a spiritualism even now, here on earth. Individuals and groups who practise these rigours end up opening themselves little by little to an exasperated sensuality which, almost as nature's vindication, takes the place of *ascesi*: because the body is 'spiritual' all becomes licit, holy. Everything is holy!

iii) The lack of respect for the times of Christ and the Father. It is a temptation that appears at the beginning of Acts, with the apostles provoking the hard response of Jesus: 'It is not for you to know the times or seasons which the Father has fixed by his own authority' (*1:7*).

All forms of millennialism or of eschatalogism are born out of the pretext of bending the designs of God to our own. Thus we can think of the many sects which preach an imminent end to the world, such as the Jehovah's Witnesses.

In conclusion, Paul exhorts us to heed all these errors, subtle but recurring in the history of the Church, even if they do not always have strong or very deviant expression. The presbyter, the one responsible, he who has the gift of synthesis and who must be attentive to the whole, is called to guard himself from them and to seize them in the community where their first seeds sprout.

Passionate and personalised alertness

'Therefore, be alert, remembering that for three years I did not cease day or night to admonish every one with tears' (*v 31*).

Paul recommends a passionate alertness, going as far as personalised tears for each one. 'Each one', *hena hekaston*, 'I did not cease to admonish with tears' says the Greek text.

It is therefore an alertness that touches the person, a spiritual rapport, because the possible errors that we have considered are born out of spiritual exuberance and not out of indifference or secularism.

I think it would be useful to amplify the apostle's exhortation at the end of the discourse of Miletus with two classical texts which constitute the 'commitment' to the presbyters. We have already cited them, but I will give them to you again for further reflection: 'Take heed to yourself and to your teaching; hold to that, for by so doing you will save both yourself and your hearers.' We find again the didactic: you/others, your teaching/those who listen. 'Till I come, attend to the public reading of scripture, to preaching, to teaching. Do not neglect the gift you have' (1 Timothy 4:16).

We can translate it in concrete terms: heed your daily meditation, especially in the form of the *lectio divina*; heed spiritual direction, confession, the moments of desert or solitude. It is in fact our spiritual application which keeps our discernment alive.

Be alert also for others, in accordance with the exhortation given in 2 Timothy 4:1-5: 'I charge you in the presence of God and of Christ Jesus who is to judge the living and the dead, and by his appearing and his kingdom, preach the word, persist in season and out of season, convince, rebuke, and exhort; be unfailing in patience and in teaching. For the time is coming when people will not accept sound teaching, but will gather for themselves teachers to their own liking, and, will turn away from listening to the truth and wander into myths.' This clarifies the Pauline parenesis in our passage of Acts.

In 2 Timothy 3:14-15, the apostle gives advice that goes beyond all the particular exhortations, and which we can express in the following terms: errors — at least the seed of them — infiltrate all ages and all cultures, making it necessary to pay constant attention to Christ and to the Church.

These are the two fundamental points of reference for constantly recentreing our presbyterial service so that we will not be blinded or led astray by discourses which seem spiritual but are not pertinent, discourses that distract, scatter or distort.

a) *Attentiveness to Christ:* a decisive point is to be alert with a nuptial love, above all through intense, intimate prayer, through adoration, so that we cultivate the sense of belonging to Jesus, even with that consolation of praying which gives a taste for this belonging. Such christological concentration is useful against all forms of artificial mediation. It will also be helped by our *lectio divina* which shows us Jesus in his singularity and in the fullness of the divinity which lives bodily in him. God has been given to us in Jesus and God is enough for us!

b) *Attentiveness to the Church:* we must love the local Church, our portion of the Church, our community, our fellow priests.

Paul exhorts us not to trust those who give us glimpses of other paths of salvation that take us away from our Church, and he invites us to welcome willingly all the helps which are found in it. We must therefore cultivate communion with our fellow priests, even in simple ways, because it is solid, enduring, capable of nourishing our life with perseverance.

These are important invitations, since the apostle affirms that what is at stake here is not only some quality of Christian service but the very being of the Church, and the reality of her relationship with Christ. After having reflected these past days on the years lived since ordination until now and after having let our apostolic consciousness of the present emerge, I think that we can receive Paul's invitation as a serious 'commitment'.

Illumine us, Lord, and keep our eyes open and awake so that we may recognise you in the midst of the imaginings of the night and in the morning mists; that we may be able to distinguish you from a multitude of imposters. We ask this through the intercession of Paul, model of bishops and priests.

12

The Way of Mercy and Pardon

Homily of the Mass for Friday, 31st Week of the Year

When we have understood the importance of the New Testament theme of being alert it is easier for us to grasp the incisive eschatology of much of the gospels without, however, arriving at the exaggerations of the theory of Loisy or of the modernists who, at the beginning of our century, considered an eschatological interpretation to be the only possible one for the Jesus event.

Never the less, in our reading and reflection on the various passages, we should remember that all the New Testament writers are pervaded by the eschatological judgement.

The parable of the dishonest steward

Today's gospel (Luke 16:1-8) is a difficult text, singular, quite enigmatic: the parable of the dishonest steward which is recorded only by Luke. It is certainly linked into an eschatological framework because the following verse, which the liturgy does not offer, says: 'Make friends for yourselves by means of unrighteous Mammon, so that when it fails they may receive you into the eternal habitations' *(16:9)*. The parable of the rich man and Lazarus follows.

Let us therefore read it in the anagogical sense, that is in relation to the situation of a person face-to-face with the imminence of the kingdom of God.

In that way we can better emphasise the word 'steward', in Greek *oikonomos,* in its profound significance: the one who takes care of the house, the one in charge, the apostle or presbyter.

We find this term where Jesus, answering Peter, says, 'Who then is the faithful and wise steward, whom his master will set over his household, to give them their portion of food at the proper time? Blessed is that servant whom his master when he comes will find so doing' *(12:42-43).*

Another link between our gospel passage and the figure of the presbyter upon whom we have been meditating can be found in the words 'Turn in the account [*apodos ton logon*] of your stewardship' *(16:2).* Give an account of the goods that were placed in your hands. Thus the author of Hebrews describes the duty of those in charge when he says to the faithful: 'Obey your leaders and submit to them for they are keeping watch over your souls, as men who will have to give account' [*hōs logon apodōsontes*] *(Hebrews 13:17).* And the apostle adds: 'Let them do this joyfully — and not sadly, for that would be of no advantage to you.'

If it is true that we are all called to give an account of ourselves, of what we have and what we do, it is all the more reason that those vested in authority should be the first to be judged. The wisdom books warn us that the judgement of God is heavy for the king and for all those who have responsibility for others.

This theme was very much to the fore in the minds of

the saints: some pages of St Charles Borromeo and of Blessed Cardinal Ferrari are actually filled with anguish over the consciousness of having to give an account of the souls for whom they are responsible. It is true that in the discourse of Miletus Paul affirms that he left nothing undone, that he never avoided that which could be useful for the community, but the figure of Paul is probably a bit idealised in Acts; Luke wanted to affirm his indisputable, admirably serious attitude towards responsibility.

All the same, the apostle did not dare to give such a judgement of himself: 'It is the Lord who judges me' *(1 Corinthians 4:4)*.

The reflection on the responsibility of the presbyter returns in the parable of the talents (Matthew 25:14-30) and in the parable of the pounds (Luke 19:11-27). Talents are the personal gifts that have been given to us; but it is a much greater responsibility to have people given us to educate in hope, in love, in liberty. We will have to render an account of whether we have multiplied the pounds, whether we have helped people to grow, or have held them in a subjection which blocked them, made them rigid, prevented them from becoming mature and authentic.

The way of mercy and pardon
The fear of responsibility therefore needs correctives to balance it.

The first, called to mind by the parable of the talents, is the joy of God (Matthew 25:21): 'Well done, good and faithful servant; you have been faithful over a little, I will set you over much; enter into the joy of your master.'

The second comes from the knowledge of being mere collaborators of the Lord, who is prince of shepherds. We are shepherds in relation to him who primarily carries the responsibility, who works in the hearts of people.

The third corrective is charity, which calls down the pardon of God. The parable of the wicked administrator provokes this from Jesus: 'And I tell you make friends for yourselves by means of unrighteous mammon' *(Luke 16:9)* even with unjust money; the more direct allusion is to temporal charity. There is, however, apostolic charity, that continuous exercise of mercy and patience, which overflows the measure of love and which causes the Lord to forgive us much. The Lord will forgive us much if we have forgiven our brothers and sisters much, not, naturally, if we are too indulgent or frivolous but if we have truly loved those who disappointed us, who caused us to despair, and perhaps who criticised us.

How desirable is this capacity of never becoming bitter, never going back over the hurts received, whether true or presumed. To forgive those who hurt us is like putting a mountain in place of a hole: it will fill it and elevate it.

A community is fraternal when the shepherd is the first not to hold grudges and does not allow the rudeness that he has received to weigh upon others, when he willingly appreciates all the efforts that are made, even if he was not their source and they were done for other motives.

Even if we don't have many gifts each of us can be generous with love and with forgiveness, in imitation of the strange steward who is praised for having known how to be generous with the little he had. We are all able to put ourselves in that situation in which God must forgive us, must cordially embrace us because we have almost preceded him in forgiveness: 'Forgive us our trespasses as we forgive those who trespass against us.' The invocation of the *Our Father* seems to say that we are the first to forgive, because the Lord at the final judgement will thus forgive us our sins.

A fraternal community is constructed above all with patience, mercy, true reconciliation with ourselves and with our brothers and sisters. There are truly zealous and generous pastors who are not reconciled with their own community, perhaps because of past disappointments and bitternesses. The people become aware of it and although they recognise their pastors as priests who are culturally well-prepared and good at preaching, they feel separated from them.

May the intercession of St Paul help us to follow the way of mercy and pardon, because it will be for our own benefit and it will make our community grow.

13

The Mystery of the Church in the Life and Ministry of the Priest

'And now I commend you to God and to the word of his grace, which is able to build you up and to give you the inheritance among all those who are sanctified. I coveted no one's silver or gold or apparel. You yourselves know that these hands ministered to my necessities, and to those who were with me. In all things I have shown you that by so toiling one must help the weak, remembering the words of the Lord Jesus, how he said "It is more blessed to give than to receive." And when he had spoken thus he knelt down and prayed with them all. And they all wept and embraced Paul and kissed him, sorrowing most of all because of the words he had spoken, that they should see his face no more. And they brought him to the ship.' (Acts 20:32-38)

We can use these last words of Paul both as a conclusion to our retreat and as an introduction to the meditation.

Commending to the Lord

'And now I commend you to the Lord.' At the end of a spiritual retreat there are usually recommendations, giving so-called reminders. I have always found it difficult to follow this custom because I am convinced that what is important for each person is to follow the reflections born of one's own consciousness, the prayer of the heart. As far as I am concerned the words of the apostle express it well: I commend you to the Lord, I commend each of you to the Lord. These words are beautiful because they recall the cry of Jesus from the cross when he recited Psalm 31: 'Father, into your hands I commend my spirit' *(Psalm 31:5)*.

Jesus entrusts his life to the Father in the certainty that it is in good hands. Paul does the same before leaving the community. We read this, for example, in Acts 14, when he is getting ready to leave for Pamphylia after having consoled and exhorted the disciples of Lystra, Iconium and Antioch: 'And when they had appointed elders for them in every church, with prayer and fasting, they committed them to the Lord in whom they believed.' (v *23*)

In this way Paul frees himself from that anxiety which we sometimes feel within us for those we have tried to guide, those whom we love. We risk keeping them tied to us when it is time for them to walk alone, to act freely.

Here the post-apostolic Church is born, at the moment at which the apostle has the courage to detach himself. On the other hand, there is no real Christian pastoral if it does not generate liberty, if the priest thinks that because he has to go on to another field of ministry, those who were confided to his care will not be able to make it alone and he therefore continues to worry about them and to pursue them with telephone calls, letters and visits to their homes.

Detachment is not indifference but an expression of faith. I commend you to God who will guide you much better than I did or would be able to do. This is an expression of faith and is authentic apostolic paternity.

'And to the word of his grace'

Paul's addition of these words has a precise sense: they do not speak of commending the word of grace to the presbyters but, rather, of commending the presbyters to the word. What does this mean? First of all the expression immediately recalls the 'gospel of grace' to which the apostle is witness (Acts 20:24). It is the first word coming forth from the mouth of Jesus, that of the New Covenant: 'And he began to say to them: "Today this Scripture has been fulfilled in your hearing." And all spoke well of him and wondered at the words of grace which proceeded out of his mouth...' *(Luke 4:21-22).*

It is the proclamation of the mercy of God towards the sinner: in spite of everything, God is on my side; he is favourable to me here and now. And this word is accomplished because it is the active power of salvation for all who believe; it is the promise already carried out right now.

We can say then that Paul truly responds to the question that is in the heart of the presbyters, of those elders of Ephesus who ask themselves how they can go on without the apostle; how they will withstand the attack of the 'fierce wolves'; how they will manage to spread this word of grace which they have partly understood yet are fearful of losing.

It is not the word that is commended to the presbyters. The word is carried out in them, rendering them suitable ministers of the New Testament, of the spirit that gives life and not the letter that kills. The strength comes from God even though we bear this treasure in earthen vessels (cf. 2 Corinthians 4:7). The word of grace carries us, frees us, fills us; it is within us. We must simply give it room and make it ever more our own in heart and mind, because it is the promise that the Lord will be merciful to us —

to me, the priest.

The word of God signifies all of this. It is not therefore a type of illuminism but an infallible gift which transforms and brings about our communion with the Trinity. If we trust this word, we can be sure that it will never fail us because it is the first determining movement of our fundamental religious conversion to which we must return continually. The power of grace is on my side, it sustains me in spite of my sins, my defects, my frailty.

The power of grace
Desiring that the *episkopoi* with whom he is speaking will not doubt the word of grace Paul explains that it 'is able to build you up and to give you the inheritance among all those who are sanctified' *(Acts 20:32)*.

We notice here the deep preoccupation of the *presbyteroi:* 'How will we build up the community? Will we build it in an authentic way or will we be among those who build houses of straw and wood, of disconnected bricks that fall at the first earthquake? Will we save ourselves?' The apostle responds that the word can build up and 'can' signifies an actual power. The word has the power to construct the community that will be the true prelude to the inheritance of the redeemed, that will assure eternal life and the fulfilment of the messianic good we have been promised.

Paul's beautiful expression reminds us of the final doxology of the Letter to the Romans, which is often neglected; this too constitutes a useful conclusion to the retreat:

'Now to him who is able to strengthen you according to my gospel and the preaching of Jesus Christ, according to the revelation of the mystery which was kept secret for long ages but is now disclosed and through the prophetic

118

writings is made known to all nations, according to the command of the eternal God, to bring about the obedience of faith — to the only wise God be glory for ever more through Jesus Christ. Amen' *(Romans 16:25-27)*.

When the moment of reflection and of meditative tranquillity has come to an end, there is always the fear in our hearts of losing what the Lord has given us to understand, of being overwhelmed by our daily routine. All the same, the power of God which stimulated us during these days will sustain us. Even our commitment of fidelity cannot be programmed, but can only be hoped for from this same grace and mercy. Thus the Christian is always brought back to the frontiers of faith and hope; it is to there that we must move, letting ourselves be consumed, preparing ourselves for the definitive sacrifice of the total gift of self.

The evangelical poverty of the priest

1. Now Paul goes back to themes already expressed because they are dear to his heart. He confesses what, as we already mentioned at the beginning, is quite usual in the words of a testament: 'I coveted no one's silver or gold or apparel'. (v *33*)

It is a splendid confession of detachment which means: in my ministry I sought nothing for myself either materially or spiritually. It is the application of evangelical poverty to the pastoral mission, which does not consist so much in seeking rigorous forms of asceticism (the life of the priest already brings with it much labour and toil) but rather in not permitting that things should attach themselves to our hands.

We know from experience that material detachment is easy enough at the beginning when we are carried along on the first wave of enthusiasm, of joyful sacrifice, of response. However, as the years pass, direct or indirect occasions arise which offer us advantages that go beyond a just reward and our real needs for the future, thus making detachment more difficult.

All the same, it is exactly when hope, abandonment and confidence begin to weaken, and tiredness and the fear of illness creep up on us, that detachment becomes more courageous, more meritorious, a real exercise of virtue.

Thank God, we have marvellous — at times even heroic — examples of this detachment, which truly edify people. Think of the many priests who, while living in an upright manner, never secretly accumulate anything for themselves or others. If the faithful are aware of this, it is because they have a profound sense of the gospel, and understand that it is here that the credibility of the priest, the apostle, the bishop is really at stake.

Spiritual detachment instead touches the heart and, as Paul says, manages even to touch the chains, the tribulations, life itself, if we are indeed slaves of Jesus. Certainly it does not concern that true affection in Christ for the persons commended to us but rather signifies that we must always beware of the spiritual *libido dominandi* that ties others to oneself in order to solve in some way one's own affective problems and needs. On an obvious level this spiritual self-interest can be easily corrected but at other more subtle and profound levels it can cause much harm to others and even to the figure of the priest. One becomes aware that he is seeking himself in the form of support, of dominion over others, because of a personal need.

2. Paul's following words are also important: 'You yourselves know that these hands ministered to my

necessities and to those who were with me' *(v 34)*.

As Ephesus was a young community with many problems and suspicions, Paul did not want to lay a financial burden on the community at the beginning of its formation, and he sought to support himself, finding time to work even though he laboured continuously at his ministry. In the same way, many of you teach and do not impose on the finances of the parish even if you have reason to do so. It is, therefore, not necessary to go to work in a factory except in particular cases which from time to time must be carefully judged.

Here that respect for the community budget that is the livelihood of many priests is emphasised; if the community can provide, it is right that it should do so (the apostle says those who work for the Gospel must also live from the Gospel; cf. 1 Corinthians 9:4). If the community is just beginning or is poor and made up of persons who do not understand, the priests should try, in every way possible, not to be a burden on them. In this regard I know of some truly heroic gestures. The new system of parish support is based above all on the contributions of the faithful, but where this is not possible it is necessary to call upon the income that the priest receives, for example from teaching religion.

In any case, it would not be right to accustom a community not to be concerned about the maintenance of the clergy. Paul, in fact, although taking into account the needs of the Church of Ephesus, reminds them that he provided for himself using words that were kindly and freeing, precisely in order to stimulate the faithful and at the same time to instruct them to be detached, to be at ease and in true freedom.

3. Then, with marvellous insight, he adds: 'In all things I have shown you that by so toiling one must help the weak' *(v 35a)*. Among the exegetes there are those who take it to mean that the weak are the poor: using the night hours to make tents, the apostle would have earned not only enough to support himself but also to help the poor of the community. Other exegetes think of those 'weak in faith': in the Church of Ephesus there were people who were mistrustful and suspicious because they came from pagan temples where the priests made a business of religion, and thus Paul would have worked also to demonstrate that his proselytism did not procure gains for him.

In any case, the expression is beautiful and corresponds to that careful detachment of which we have spoken, which flows into the evocation of the phrase of Jesus: 'remembering the words of the Lord Jesus, how he said "It is more blessed to give than to receive" ' *(v 35b)*.

The beatitude of giving

Here we have one of the pearls of scripture — the beatitude of giving. Literally, it is almost stronger than the others which cannot be compared with it: 'Blessed are the poor... Blessed are the meek... Blessed are the pure...'. That it is more blessed to give than to receive is an assertion which upsets the order of human greed. Paul uses this assertion to give a definition of humankind that can be reached only by starting with the gospel of grace, with the gratuity of God.

If, in his innermost being, God is giving, then the creature made in the image of God expresses itself in giving rather than in receiving.

This is indeed the climax of the discourse of Miletus. Never the less it is also good to receive. I want therefore to thank you for all that I have received during these days from you young priests, and for the gift that you have offered older priests.

He prayed with them all

'And when he had spoken thus he knelt down and prayed with them all.' *(v 36)*

We do not know the contents of that prayer. It is even possible that they celebrated the Eucharist together as Paul had done earlier at Troade. In that case it would have been a prayer of praise and thanksgiving to the Father, in which the apostle would have asked the Lord, for the presbyters, for the gift of serving him in all humility, of undergoing trials with courage and of growing in faith and hope while passing through tears. Paul would have continued: O Lord, do not allow them to shrink from what may be useful for preaching to the faithful and for instructing them in public and in their homes. Let them know how to help their people be converted to God and believe in the Lord Jesus Christ. Grant them the strength not to tire in their journey but to finish the course they have started, the service which you, Lord Jesus, confided to them. Grant them the grace to bear witness to the message of the grace of God.

In conclusion, I too would like to take up again in the form of prayer, each one of us for the other, at least a few of the reflections we have shared:

Grant, O Lord, that we may never shrink from the task of announcing your counsel to our people, that is, all the ways in which you want to be served.

Grant that we may heed ourselves and all the flock in the midst of whom you have set us as pastors.

Grant us the courage and discernment to defend the flock from fierce wolves; grant that we may be alert, take heed, overcome our drowsiness, and be attentive to your Spirit who speaks, to the evil spirit who tries to corrupt our children, our youth, our people.

Let us know how to exhort you with tears by day and, if necessary, by night, for each of those whom we love and whom you have commended to us.

We give you thanks, Lord, because we have confidence in you; we are in your hands. We thank you for the word of your grace which edifies this community and which alone prepares us for our eternal inheritance. Help us to look to that inheritance with confidence, because even though the future may be uncertain your grace is surely certain.

Grant us disinterest, Lord Jesus, so that we may seek neither silver, nor gold, nor the clothes of anyone and that we may not impose ourselves as masters of the heart of anyone.

Grant us detachment and the grace to work as much as is necessary to help others and to assist the poor and those weak in faith.

Grant us the grace to feel in the commitment of our daily ministry that there is more joy in giving than in receiving.

The mystery of the Church

Contemplating the scene of the elders of Ephesus who burst into tears, embraced Paul, kissed him and accompanied him as far as the ship (cf. vv. 37-38), we have a splendid image of the Church which is being formed.

I would like, however, to conclude by recalling the final words of John Paul II's encyclical, *Redemptor Hominis:*

'Therefore the Church, uniting herself with all the riches of the mystery of the Redemption, becomes the Church of living people, living because given life from within by the working of "the Spirit of truth" and visited by the love that the Holy Spirit has poured into our hearts. The aim of any service in the Church, whether the service is apostolic, pastoral, priestly or episcopal, is to keep up this dynamic link between the mystery of the Redemption and every man.

'If we are aware of this task, then we seem to understand better what it means to say that the Church is a mother and also what it means to say that the Church always, and particularly at our time, has need of a mother.... For if we feel a special need, in this difficult and responsible phase of the history of the Church and of humankind, to turn to Christ, who is Lord of the Church and Lord of human history on account of the mystery of the Redemption, we believe that nobody else can bring us as Mary can into the divine and human dimension of his mystery. Nobody has been brought into it by God himself as Mary has.... 'The special characteristic of the motherly love that the mother of God inserts in the mystery of the Redemption and the life of the Church, finds expression in its exceptional closeness to humanity and all its circumstances. It is in this that the mystery of the mother consists. The Church, which looks to her with altogether special love and hope, wishes to make this mystery her own in an ever deeper manner. For in this the Church also recognises the way for her daily life, which is each person.' (n. 22)

Let us pray for one another that this vision of the Church, whose way lies through humankind, through the intercession of Mary, mother of God and our mother, may also be expressed in our way of being and living Church, of sharing in the mystery of our mother the Church.